UAE
DAY TRIPPER

there's more to life...
askexplorer.com

UAE Day Tripper 2013/1st Edition

ISBN 978-9948-03-335-6

Front Cover Photograph – Pete Maloney

Explorer Publishing & Distribution

PO Box 34275, Dubai, United Arab Emirates

Phone   +971 (0)4 340 8805

Fax   +971 (0)4 340 8806

Email   info@askexplorer.com

Web   askexplorer.com

Welcome...

Living in the UAE means being blessed with a wealth of choice. On any given day you could find yourself having an adventure, whether that means exploring an ancient desert fort, diving with sharks or racing around a world famous Formula 1 track. The sheer amount of options can be overwhelming: where to begin?

Fortunately, Explorer has done the research so you don't have to. *UAE Day Tripper* is a round-up of the country's best day trip destinations and experiences, from world famous attractions to hidden gems discovered off the beaten track. This easy-to-read guide takes all the hassle out of planning your day and helps you make the most of your time in the UAE, whether you've got a troop of toddlers to keep entertained or a group of visiting relatives that you want to show off your city to.

UAE Day Tripper is split into different categories – including Beaches & Parks, Sights & Attractions, and Wildlife & Sealife – and divided according to emirate for easy reference. The attractions are labelled with clear icons that highlight the best places to spend a full day, soak up some sun, stay cool indoors or be entertained without spending a single dirham.

What will you do today?

We'd love to hear from you, whether you make a great insider discovery or want to share your views about this or any of our products. Fill in our reader survey at askexplorer.com/feedback – and get 20% off your next online purchase.

GET YOUR PERSEDIAN GULF ADVENTURE WITH

PRINCE OF SEA

DAILY CRUISES IN RAS AL-KHAIMAH/DUBAI

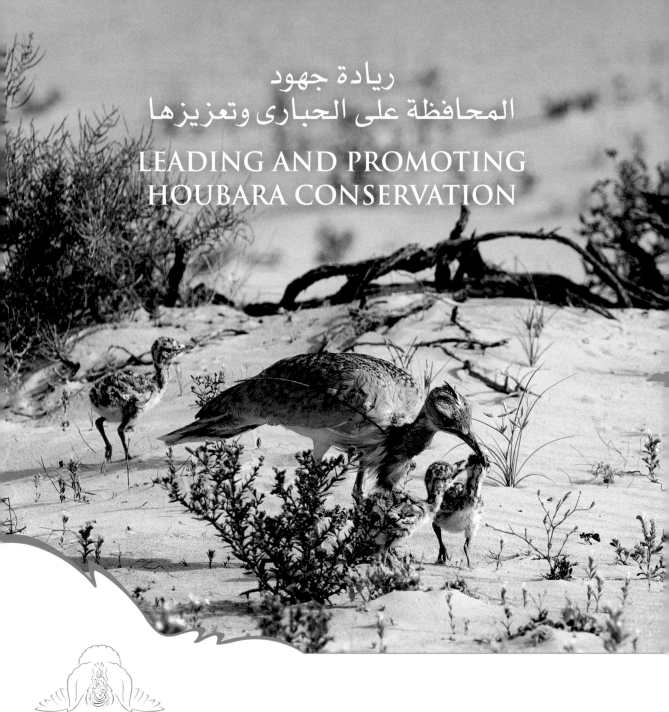

ريادة جهود
المحافظة على الحبارى وتعزيزها

LEADING AND PROMOTING
HOUBARA CONSERVATION

INTERNATIONAL FUND FOR
HOUBARA CONSERVATION

www.houbarafund.org

YellowHat Japan

One-stop centre for car accessories and services

WE SPECIALIZE...

TYRES & TYRE SERVICES

- With YellowHat Tyre Loyalty Program, We take care of your vehicle tyres till 40,000 kms

Continental • BRIDGESTONE • MICHELIN • GOODYEAR • DUNLOP • Hankook • YOKOHAMA • PIRELLI

PREMIUM DETAILING
with Paint Protection Crystal Lacquer
- Deep cleaning from interior to exterior

Up to 2 years warranty!

GTECHNIQ

OIL CHANGE

TOTAL • Mobil 1

AUDIO/VIDEO & INSTALLATION

KENWOOD • Pioneer • ALPINE • JVC • FLY AUDIO • Rockford Fosgate • Lightning Audio • MATCH • HELIX • FOC

CAR FOILING
- It gives style, beauty & protection on your car.

mactac • ORACAL • HEXIS

CAR WINDOW TINT
- Provides protection from UV rays & helps your car AC to cool easily.

3M • MADICO

Valet service available for your vehicle
We pick up... We deliver
Just give us a call
04 289 80 60
(only applicable for automobile services)

YELLOWHAT SERVICE CENTRE
NOW OPEN AT AL QUOZ
(BEHIND AL TAYER MOTORS, NEAR TIMES SQUARE CENTER)

CONTACT US
04 340 46

Nad Al Hamar - Aweer road
04 289 80 60

Times Square Center
04 341 85 92

Facebook: Yellowhat ae   www.yellowhat.ae

© Julie Remy

MEDECINS SANS FRONTIERES
أطبّــاء بــلا حــدود

unconditional
medical care where needed,
when needed

Médecins Sans Frontières (MSF, or Doctors Without Borders) is an international, independent, medical humanitarian organization that delivers emergency aid in more than 70 countries to people affected by armed conflict, epidemics, natural or man-made disasters or exclusion from healthcare.

© Lam Duc Hien

© Mads Nissen

© Sarah Elliott

© Remco Bohle

© Ton Koene

© Eddy McCall

www.msf-me.org
Abu Dhabi: P.O. Box 47226, T: +971 2 631 7645, E: office-abudhabi@msf.org
Dubai: P.O. Box 65650, T: +971 4 457 9255, E: office-dubai@msf.org

The best things in life are at Zayed Sports City! Home to over 20 sports there is something for everyone, whether you're into casual bowling, fast paced football, chilled-out ice skating or even high powered tennis matches. As the city's largest sports and recreation facility, Zayed Sports City is not to be missed on your next day out.

TABLE OF CONTENTS

WHAT SHALL WE DO TODAY?

STUCK FOR IDEAS ON WHERE TO GO AND WHAT TO DO ON YOUR DAY OFF? LET EXPLORER LEAD YOU IN THE RIGHT DIRECTION...

With so much to do and see in the UAE, it's hard to know where to start. Blessed as we are with perennial sunshine, an outdoor lifestyle and diverse landscapes, not to mention a multicultural society and a booming leisure industry, we all know we should be 'making the most of it'. But in a country full of showstopping tourist attractions it's hard to remember, or even find, the hidden gems, the cultural treasures, the great picnic spots and the places that are simply guaranteed to give the entire family a day of good, clean fun.

UAE Day Tripper is your guide to the best sights and attractions in the country – whether you've heard of them or not. It's a bank of ideas to get you inspired for those (not so) rainy days when you're at a loose end. Whether you need somewhere new to entertain the kids, feel you're due an injection of culture, or fancy something completely out of the ordinary – the answer is in these pages.

DAY TRIPPING

We've chosen attractions and activities that are accessible and often budget-friendly; places that you'll be able to head to without too much forward planning.

Each entry is listed by city and includes all the practical information you need to know – from opening times, contact details and prices to attraction highlights. We've also indicated how long you're likely to spend at each attraction, and suggested things to see and do nearby to help you make the most of your day out. We've included maps of each emirate, as well as Al Ain, to help you find your way.

INSPIRE ME

Follow the 'indoor' icon to escape the heat of summer, or the 'outdoor' icon to make the most of the winter weather; or, if you fancy some water-based activities, look out for the 'get wet' icon. Most of the attractions listed here are family-friendly, but you'll find a little extra excitement at the attractions marked 'adrenaline'.

For a morning or afternoon excursion, look for the 'short stay' icon. Or, if you're looking for somewhere to keep the kids entertained all day long, attractions marked 'full day' will do just that. Check out the table overleaf for more inspiration by location.

 Free

 Indoor

 Outdoor

 Full Day

 Short Stay

 Adrenaline

 Get Wet

WE'VE DIVIDED THE BOOK INTO CATEGORIES, AND WITHIN EACH SECTION IS A RANGE OF ATTRACTIONS TO SUIT ALL BUDGETS.

AMUSEMENT PARKS

We cover the country's superb array of water parks and theme parks, from the thrills and spills of Ice Land Water Park in Ras Al Khaimah to the more modest water-based fun of Murjan Splash Park in Abu Dhabi. Adrenaline junkies will love the world's fastest rollercoaster at Ferrari World, while there are rides for all the family at Al Ain's Hili Fun City.

BEACHES & PARKS

We guide you through our top picks for spending a day in the open air, whether by the seaside or surrounded by greenery. From miles of fabulous free beaches to the cities' nominally priced parks, there's a wealth of superb facilities to suit even the smallest budget – and you're likely to find something very close to home.

SIGHTS & ATTRACTIONS

This section is grouped into Art & Culture, Family, Forts & Mosques, Heritage Sites, Landmarks, and Museums. You'll find everything from Sharjah's multitude of top-notch educational attractions to Ajman's fantastic museum. We bring you the galleries of Dubai that are defining the city as a creative hub and Fujairah's historical forts, plus the entertainment centres all over the country that make a trip to the mall a fun family day out.

SPORTS & LEISURE

With everything from bowling and paintballing to skiing and skydiving, there's no time to get bored in the UAE. We also recommend the best places to try out watersports, such as Umm Al Quwain's placid lagoon, cableboarding at Al Forsan International Sports Resort in Abu Dhabi, or the white water rafting runs at Wadi Adventure. For venues that offer something for everyone, check out the Multi-sports section.

WILDLIFE & SEALIFE

For the chance to walk, talk and even swim with the animals, we bring you the country's best animal encounters both on land and underwater. Feed giraffes at Al Ain Zoo or swim with dolphins at Dubai Dolphinarium.

SEE P.XVIII FOR ITINERARIES BASED ON EMIRATE AND CITY, AND TO GET A SENSE OF WHAT IS ACHIEVABLE IN ONE DAY – ESPECIALLY HELPFUL IF YOU ARE VENTURING SOMEWHERE NEW.

	Free	Indoor	Outdoor	Full Day	Short Stay	Adrenaline	Get Wet	Page
ABU DHABI								
Abu Dhabi Corniche			●	●			●	p.24
Abu Dhabi Falcon Hospital		●			●			p.194
Al Forsan International Sports Resort			●			●	●	p.166
Emirates National Auto Museum		●			●			p.100
Emirates Park Zoo			●	●				p.196
Family Park			●	●				p.40
Ferrari World Abu Dhabi		●		●		●		p.2
Heritage Village			●		●			p.90
Khalifa International Bowling Centre		●			●			p.138
Manarat Al Saadiyat	●	●		●				p.58
Murjan Splash Park					●		●	p.10
Saadiyat Public Beach			●	●			●	p.26
Sheikh Zayed Grand Mosque	●	●	●		●			p.82
Sparky's Family Fun Park		●			●			p.66
Wanasa Land		●		●				p.68
Yas Marina Circuit					●	●		p.154
Yas Waterworld				●		●	●	p.12
Zayed Sports City		●	●	●				p.168
Zayed Sports City Ice Rink		●			●			p.148
AJMAN								
Ajman Corniche	●		●				●	p.28
Ajman Museum		●			●			p.102
AL AIN								
Al Ain Mall Ice Rink		●			●			p.150
Al Ain National Museum		●			●			p.104
Al Ain Oasis	●		●		●			p.42
Al Ain Palace Museum	●	●			●			p.106
Al Ain Raceway International Kart Circuit			●		●	●		p.156
Al Ain Zoo			●	●				p.198
Al Jahili Fort	●	●			●			p.84
Al Jahili Park	●		●		●			p.44
Hili Archaeological Park			●		●			p.108
Hili Fun City			●	●		●		p.4
Wadi Adventure			●			●	●	p.170

	Free	Indoor	Outdoor	Full Day	Short Stay	Adrenaline	Get Wet	Page
DUBAI								
Adventure HQ		●			●			p.144
Al Fahidi Historical Neighbourhood			●	●				p.60
Al Nasr Leisureland			●				●	p.172
Alserkal Avenue		●		●				p.62
Aquaplay					●		●	p.70
Aquaventure				●		●	●	p.14
Bowling City		●			●			p.140
Children's City		●		●				p.72
Creek Park			●	●				p.46
Dubai Aquarium & Underwater Zoo		●			●			p.186
Dubai Kartdrome & Autodrome		●	●			●		p.158
Dubai Dolphinarium		●			●		●	p.188
Dubai Ice Rink		●			●			p.152
Dubai Moving Image Museum		●			●			p.110
Dubai Museum		●			●			p.112
Downtown Dubai		●	●	●				p.98
Emirates Kart Zone			●		●	●		p.160
Heritage & Diving Villages			●		●			p.92
iFLY Dubai		●			●	●		p.178
JBR Beach	●		●				●	p.30
JA Jebel Ali Golf Resort			●	●			●	p.162
Jumeirah Beach Park			●	●			●	p.32
Jumeirah Mosque		●			●			p.86
Kids Connection		●			●			p.74
KidZania				●				p.76
Kitesurfers' Beach			●	●			●	p.34
Little Explorers		●		●				p.78
The Lost Chambers Aquarium		●			●			p.190
Magic Planet		●		●				p.80
Mamzar Beach Park			●	●	●		●	p.36
Miracle Garden			●		●			p.48
Mushrif Park			●	●				p.50
Playnation		●			●			p.146
Safa Park			●	●				p.52

	Free	Indoor	Outdoor	Full Day	Short Stay	Adrenaline	Get Wet	Page
SEGA Republic		●				●		p.6
Sheikh Saeed Al Maktoum House		●			●			p.114
Ski Dubai		●				●		p.176
Switch Bowling Dubai		●			●			p.142
Tee & Putt		●			●			p.164
Umm Suqeim Beach			●	●			●	p.38
Watercooled		●				●	●	p.180
Wild Wadi Water Park			●			●	●	p.16
Zabeel Park		●	●					p.54
FUJAIRAH								
Fujairah Fort	●				●			p.88
Fujairah Heritage Village		●			●			p.94
Fujairah Museum		●			●			p.116
RAS AL KHAIMAH								
Ice Land Water Park			●	●		●	●	p.18
National Museum Of Ras Al Khaimah		●			●			p.118
SHARJAH								
Adventureland		●				●		p.8
Al Tamimi Stables			●	●				p.200
Arabia's Wildlife Centre		●			●			p.202
Sharjah Aquarium		●			●			p.192
Sharjah Archaeology Museum		●			●			p.120
Sharjah Art Museum		●			●			p.64
Sharjah Classic Car Museum		●			●			p.122
Sharjah Discovery Centre		●			●			p.124
Sharjah Golf & Shooting Club		●	●		●			p.174
Sharjah Heritage Area		●	●		●			p.96
Sharjah Heritage Museum		●			●			p.126
Sharjah Maritime Museum		●			●			p.128
Sharjah Museum Of Islamic Civilization		●			●			p.130
Sharjah Natural History & Botanical Museum		●			●			p.132
Sharjah Science Museum		●			●			p.134
UMM AL QUWAIN								
Dreamland Aqua Park			●			●	●	p.20
UAQ Marine Club		●	●				●	p.182

ABU DHABI

Abu Dhabi is well and truly on the map as a city with more than its share of must-see attractions. While the city centre is home to a charming Corniche and some family-friendly parks, its surrounding islands are establishing themselves as entertainment and cultural hubs. Yas Island in particular is a destination in its own right, thanks to adrenaline pumping theme parks Yas Waterworld and Ferrari World, as well as Yas Marina Circuit, the formidable home of the Abu Dhabi Grand Prix.

If Yas Island is the ultimate destination for adrenaline junkies, then Saadiyat Island is made for culture vultures. With the openings of a Louvre and a Guggenheim in the next few years, it will become a cultural cornerstone. In the meantime, Manarat al Saadiyat hosts some fascinating exhibitions.

Over on the main island, the capital's gorgeous beaches and bustling Corniche are perfect for whiling away a sunny afternoon.

CULTURE

MORNING: Soak up the architectural magnificence of Sheikh Zayed Grand Mosque with an informative guided tour.

AFTERNOON: Head for Saadiyat Island to browse the exhibitions at Manarat al Saadiyat and find out about the future Louvre Abu Dhabi and Guggenheim Abu Dhabi. Enjoy lunch at Fanr, a foodie-friendly, arty cafe.

FULL DAY

MORNING: Spend the day getting wet and wild at record-breaking Yas Waterworld on Yas Island.

LUNCH: Rent out one of the air-conditioned cabanas and enjoy your own food and drinks menu.

AFTERNOON: Entertain the kids on the PearlMasters Treasure Hunt – head to the souk to get started.

INDOOR

MORNING: Get the adrenaline pumping at Ferrari World on Yas Island.

AFTERNOON: In keeping with the motorsports theme, visit the Emirates National Auto Museum.

OUTDOOR

MORNING: Head for BAKE beach club on Saadiyat Island, where you can relax on sun loungers and even try your hand at some kayaking or stand up paddleboarding.

AFTERNOON: Take a stroll along Abu Dhabi Corniche and round off your day with impeccable seafood at La Mer in the Sofitel.

AJMAN

As the smallest of the UAE's seven emirates, Ajman is sometimes overlooked. However, its more manageable size makes it much easier to navigate and, despite being less than an hour's drive from most other emirates, Ajman's city centre has a far more relaxed mood than its bustling neighbours. Plus, what it lacks in skyscraper valleys and gargantuan theme parks, it more than makes up for with peaceful, family-friendly beaches, impressive cultural attractions, and a surprising dining scene that boasts some culinary gems.

FAMILY

MORNING: Take a stroll along the Corniche, grab some ice cream at one of the cafes, browse the stalls and soak up the sun while admiring the view of the Gulf.
LUNCH: Have fresh seafood cooked to order at the excellent Themar al Bahar.
AFTERNOON: Visit Ajman City Centre for some shopping and noisy fun at Magic Planet followed by a trip to the cinema.

FULL DAY

MORNING: Spend the morning taking in the exhibitions at the Ajman Museum. Follow it with a trip to the fish market where you can see traditional fishing boats and pick up some fresh catch to have cooked and seasoned on site.
AFTERNOON: Head to the Corniche to sunbathe or try your hand at some watersports. Round off the day with a delicious authentic Indian meal at the Kempinski's Bukhara restaurant.

CULTURE

MORNING: Visit Al Tallah Camel Racecourse; although there is no official timetable, races normally take place on weekend mornings, with additional races on public holidays – and it's best to get there early.
LUNCH: Visit Attibrah on Corniche Road for delicious and authentic Emirati cuisine in a beautifully evocative setting.
AFTERNOON: Round off the day with shisha on the terrace at Arajeel as you watch the Corniche liven up with the early evening buzz.

AL AIN

When you need a rest from the bustle of the city, but don't want to have to board planes or cross borders to find it, Al Ain offers the perfect solution. The Garden City, as it's also known, is just a 90-minute drive from Dubai (and even easier to reach from Abu Dhabi). However, its green oases, wide open spaces, historic forts and palaces, and rugged mountain backdrop make it seem a world away.

Al Ain is an outdoor enthusiast's paradise that really comes into its own during the cooler months. Jebel Hafeet, the highest peak in the UAE, towers over the border between Al Ain and Oman at an imposing 1,240 metres. If you're feeling adventurous,

the gruelling Jebel Hafeet Mountain Road to the top is a popular route with runners and cyclists – and you'll be rewarded with exhilarating views. Alternatively, the winding 13km road to the peak is widely regarded as one of the best driving roads in the world.

For adrenaline junkies who want to take on more than the landscape, water-based activity centre Wadi Adventure boasts plenty of man-made challenges. The city has several relaxing, family-friendly activities too: Al Ain Zoo is a sprawling outdoor wonderland that feels more like a safari park, and Hili Fun City has an ideal mix of white-knuckle rides and green spaces to relax.

OUTDOOR
MORNING: Head for Wadi Adventure and tackle the white water rafting and kayaking runs, surf pool or challenging airpark. There are restaurants and cafes on-site for grabbing a spot of lunch.
AFTERNOON: Hop in the car and take the winding scenic drive to the top of Jebel Hafeet and admire the views.

FULL DAY
MORNING: Soak up the atmosphere at the camel and livestock souk near the Balwadi Mall complex.
LUNCH: Enjoy authentic Lebanese cuisine at Al Rikab restaurant, located at Al Ain Equestrian Centre.
AFTERNOON: Stroll through the lush palms at Al Ain Oasis, visit Al Ain Palace Museum, and finish off at the striking Al Jahili Fort across the road.

FAMILY
MORNING: Walk on the wild side with a visit to Al Ain Zoo.
AFTERNOON: Pick up a picnic lunch and head for Hili Fun City. Relax on the shaded lawns before braving some of the theme park rides.

DUBAI

While New York may be 'the city that never sleeps', Dubai is surely the city that never stops. The attractions and activities on offer here read like an adventurer's ultimate bucket list. Where else in the world can you skydive and ski, paddleboard, surf and snorkel, go kart and swim with dolphins – all in one day, if you were so inclined?

And when it's time to unwind and indulge, you'll find world-class luxury resorts right on your doorstep.

Then there's the other side of Dubai; the part that exists away from the skyscraper valleys. On the banks of the Dubai Creek, you can wander around long-established heritage areas such as Al Fahidi Historical Neighbourhood (formerly Bastakiya), see traditional architecture, sample authentic cuisine, and learn about life before the discovery of oil. The ornate mosques and traditional souks in Deira are unmissable, and an abra trip across the Creek will get you there from just Dhs.1.

ADRENALINE

MORNING: Defy gravity: choose iFLY Dubai for indoor skydiving or go bungee jumping at Gravity Zone.
LUNCH: Try the cracking seafood at Aprons and Hammers, Mina Seyahi Beach Resort.
AFTERNOON: Head to SEGA Republic for the fast and furious mechanical tornado ride, XYCLONE, and more.

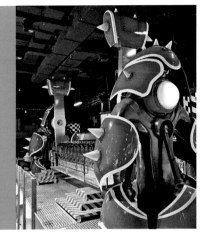

FULL DAY

MORNING: Spend the day making a splash at Aquaventure.
LUNCH: Break for lunch by the beach at Nasimi.
AFTERNOON: Pop into The Lost Chambers Aquarium for an underwater odyssey.

CULTURE

MORNING: Take a tour of Jumeirah Mosque followed by a visit to the Sheikh Mohammed Bin Rashid Centre for Cultural Understanding for a traditional Emirati lunch.
AFTERNOON: Explore the Al Fahidi Historical Neighbourhood (formerly Bastakiya) and take an abra across Dubai Creek to haggle in the souks.

INDOOR

MORNING: Hit the slopes and make 'Peng Friends' at Ski Dubai.
LUNCH: Indulge in Tex Mex egg rolls and Oreo milkshakes at The Cheesecake Factory.
AFTERNOON: Brave the Sky Trail at Adventure HQ.

FUJAIRAH

With the rugged Hajar Mountains stretching parallel to the gorgeous Gulf of Oman, Fujairah is an incredibly picturesque place to spend the day. Whether you head straight for a deserted public beach with a picnic and a cricket bat, or opt to explore the mountains, wadis and historical forts of the interior, it's the landscape that is the main draw of Fujairah. You'll be rewarded with waterfalls, natural hot springs, and the kind of peace and quiet you would never find in the neighbouring cities.

The beaches of the east coast are beautiful stretches of clean, undeveloped sand, and make for a great watersports destination. Several companies offer diving and snorkelling trips to explore the reefs of popular dive sites such as Snoopy Island.

Fujairah town itself is a mix of old and new, with cultural treasures to be found at Fujairah Museum and Fujairah Heritage Village. Forts and watchtowers dotted around the emirate are good reasons to venture into the mountainous terrain.

FULL DAY
Head to Al Aqah public beach with your snorkelling gear and swim out to Snoopy Island. Pack a picnic and enjoy a BBQ lunch by the waves.

CULTURE
MORNING: Stop at the Friday Market before visiting Fujairah Fort and Fujairah Museum. **AFTERNOON:** Wander around Fujairah Heritage Village, and take a dip in one the spring-fed swimming pools.

FAMILY
FULL DAY: Head to Fujairah City Centre to entertain the kids with games at Magic Planet, followed by a movie at the cinema.

OUTDOOR
Experience the emirate's rugged landscape with a drive through Wadi Hayl to Al Hayl Fort and beyond. Set aside time to explore pools, fertile oases and mountains along the way.

RAS AL KHAIMAH

A visit to the 'top of the tent' is an adventure into some of the best scenery in the country. With the Hajar Mountains rising dramatically behind the city, fantastic dunes to explore and the Arabian Gulf stretching out to the fore, Ras Al Khaimah is a condensed version of the best of the UAE.

Here you'll find peaceful developments with great restaurants and shopping, the all-out fun of Ice Land Water Park, and watersports all along the coast.

RAK's town is quiet and relaxing, with a serene and striking mangrove habitat at its heart, and there are a number of ancient sites nearby that are well worth investigating.

FULL DAY
MORNING: Start your day by embarking from Al Hamra Marine & Yacht Club for a full day cruise aboard the Prince of Sea yacht and set sail for Al Marjan Island, where you try out various watersports like snorkelling, kayaking and speedboat rides.
LUNCH: Enjoy a buffet lunch on the waves.
AFTERNOON: Relax and unwind aboard the Prince of Sea – soak up some sun and lounge on the deck, listening to music as you sail home.

CULTURE
MORNING: Visit the Pearl Museum and stroll along Al Qawasim Corniche.
LUNCH: Feast at Pesto Ristorante, followed by shisha on the rooftop.
AFTERNOON: Spend time at the National Museum of Ras Al Khaimah, then drive out to Dhayah Fort.

SHARJAH

As the cultural heart of the UAE, Sharjah's museums, heritage attractions and science centres are arguably the best in the country. It is also an extremely family-friendly emirate, with many of its cultural treasures geared towards engaging and entertaining children as well as adults.

Attractions in Sharjah are grouped into handy clusters, making a day trip surprisingly easy to handle. For a sense of what Sharjah is all about, head towards Khalid Lagoon to enjoy the peace and calm of this waterfront emirate. Close to each other at the south end of the lagoon are the social hubs of Al Majaz Waterfront and Al Qasba, where alfresco, waterside dining complements children's play areas and unique attractions.

The beautifully restored Heart of Sharjah, where you can gain a sense of the Sharjah of old, comprises traditional houses, coral alleyways, windtowers and cobbled squares, as well as a multitude of well-curated museums, landmarks and an old souk.

Away from the bustle of the city, on the Sharjah-Dhaid road, are a number of accessible, quality attractions covering science, archaeology, classic cars and Arabian wildlife.

FAMILY
MORNING: Head to Arabia's Wildlife Centre at Sharjah Desert Park.
LUNCH: Grab a tasty homemade curry at the centre's great cafe.
AFTERNOON: Feed the animals at the Children's Farm and then move on to the Sharjah Natural History and Botanical Museum.

INDOOR
MORNING: Have fun at the Discovery Centre and Sharjah Science Museum.
AFTERNOON: Visit Sharjah Classic Cars Museum.

CULTURE
MORNING: Explore Sharjah Aquarium and Sharjah Maritime Museum in Al Khan.
LUNCH: Take your pick of the cafes and restaurants at Al Qasba and enjoy an alfresco lunch by the canal, then have a ride on the Eye of the Emirates ferris wheel.
AFTERNOON: Enjoy a wander around the Heart of Sharjah: haggling at Souk Al Arsah and taking in Sharjah Heritage Museum, Sharjah Art Museum, the Creek and the Museum of Islamic Civilisation.

UMM AL QUWAIN

Home to the UAE's most established water park, Umm Al Quwain has been drawing in tourists for years. But the day trippers that come here do so for the same reason they did 20 years ago – the quiet, laidback pace and the acres of serene marshy lagoon and mangrove habitats.

Most of the activities in Umm Al Quwain are centred around its budget-friendly resorts, but you don't have to stay overnight to book. Boat trips, windsurfing and other watersports are available. Barracuda Beach Resort is perhaps the most popular, with a tax-free drinks emporium and a lovely gourmet food shop. UAQ Marine Club is great for watersports, while Flamingo Beach Resort hosts the unusual sport of crab hunting.

FAMILY

Head to Dreamland Aqua Park and take on the terrifying Kamikaze and Black Hole, before floating along the lazy river. Parents can have lunch at the licensed pool bar and unwind with a shisha.

FULL DAY

Spend the day at UAQ Marine Club. Kayak through the gorgeous mangroves or try some more adrenaline-pumping watersports such as wakeboarding, then have lunch and relax by the pool. Stock up at Barracuda Beach Resort before returning home.

Come Play for The Day at Atlantis, The Palm

ATLANTIS
THE PALM, DUBAI
~ **ENDLESS WONDER**

Release the thrill-seeker in you with **NEW** record breaking rides at **Aquaventure Waterpark,** the No.1 waterpark in the Middle East and Europe.

Rediscover the explorer in you at **The Lost Chambers Aquarium**, home to a mythical lost city and 65,000 amazing marine animals

Make a new friend at **Dolphin Bay**. Experience a close encounter that you'll treasure for a lifetime.

Book today on atlantisthepalm.com for the best available rates

*Proof of UAE residency required. Resident rate not applicable for Dolphin Bay.

Amusement Parks

FERRARI WORLD ABU DHABI

WHERE Yas Island West
WHEN Daily, 11am-8pm
HOW MUCH Dhs.240
(general admission)
TIME SPENT Full day
CONTACT 02 496 8000
WEBSITE ferrariworldabudhabi.com
MAP p.209

For high-speed thrills that can be enjoyed even during the stifling summer months, where better to go than the world's largest indoor theme park? Ferrari World Abu Dhabi is just that; part F1 amusement park and part museum dedicated to the Italian supercar, this attraction has won the hearts of the UAE's petrolheads and visitors alike. There's plenty to keep kids entertained, as well as rides for teen and adult adrenaline junkies.

One of the highlights is undoubtedly Formula Rossa – billed as the world's fastest rollercoaster, it reaches such high speeds (up to 240kmph) that anyone adventurous enough to give

it a go has to wear goggles. There's a flume-style water ride based on the twists and turns of a Ferrari engine, state-of-the-art simulators to recreate the experience of a real Grand Prix, and a thrilling 62m high ride that drops vertically through the park's roof. For younger visitors, there are gentler rides and attractions at the Junior Training Camp.

If a full day of rides seems too much, take a break with a tour of a miniature Italy, a multimedia journey through racing history, and stop to admire the display of Ferrari cars – before picking up a souvenir sporting the famous 'prancing horse' logo!

BEST FOR **Visitors**

HIGHLIGHTS
Formula Rossa rollercoaster
Galleria Ferrari displays
Junior Training Camp for kids

NEARBY ATTRACTIONS
Try a driving experience at Yas Marina Circuit, or head to Yas Waterworld for more adrenaline-pumping fun.

"Brave Formula Rossa, the world's fastest rollercoaster."

HILI FUN CITY

WHERE Off Emirates St
WHEN Timings vary
HOW MUCH From Dhs.50
TIME SPENT Full day
CONTACT 03 784 5542
WEBSITE hilifuncity.ae
MAP p.210

From white-knuckle thrillers to toddler-sized attractions, there's something for everyone to explore and enjoy in the leafy grounds of Hili Fun City. This recently renovated theme park offers visitors the best of both worlds: an amusement park packed with rides and activities, and a scenic picnic spot for more relaxed get-togethers with friends.

It's best to arrive early and make a day of it. There are more than 30 attractions, ranging from gentle rides for the little ones – such as the zebra-striped safari jeeps and Hili Express train – to nail-biting, high-flying rides for teens and adults, like the terrifying Sky Flyer that spins you round 360 degrees. For more traditional entertainment, take a seat in the amphitheatre, where singing, dancing and circus shows are staged throughout the day. Alternatively, enjoy some daredevil action with your feet firmly on the ground at the 3D Action Cinema; it's the perfect place to escape the heat of the midday sun.

Take a pedal boat ride on the lake, hire a bike and explore the grounds, or take the risk of getting wet on the bumper boats. For a relaxing pit-stop, go prepared with sandwiches and cake and enjoy a picturesque picnic in the shade of a tree.

HIGHLIGHTS
Sky Flyer rollercoaster
Hili Express train ride
3D Action Cinema

NEARBY ATTRACTIONS
For a family day out, divide your time between a visit to Hili Fun City and a trip to see the animals at the excellent Al Ain Zoo.

"Hire a cycle for up to six people, and explore the park on wheels."

SEGA REPUBLIC

WHERE The Dubai Mall, Level 2
WHEN Weekdays, 10am-11pm
Weekends, 10am-midnight
HOW MUCH Dhs.600 for Family
Power Pass (day pass for four people)
TIME SPENT Full day
CONTACT 04 448 8484
WEBSITE segarepublic.com
MAP p.214

BEST FOR
Families

Don't be fooled by the somewhat dated, amusement arcade feel to this indoor theme park in The Dubai Mall – SEGA Republic is really, really fun and, unlike many other shopping mall amusement centres, is for all ages.

Big kids as well as little ones will find enough thrills and spills to satisfy, with some familiar characters for company: escape evil Dr. Eggman on the rotating rollercoaster in the dark, SpinGear; be dropped from a height on the Sonic Hopper; and get flung around on Robotnik. There are some genuinely unique rides at SEGA Republic, including the dizzying Halfpipe Canyon, which sees you working your 'snowboard' to spin higher and faster in order to beat your opponent, and the stomach-flipping Storm-G, which feels like a regular racing game until you're spun completely upside down. Enjoy a stomach-churning virtual flight through the jungle in the motion-simulator Wild Jungle, or brave the House of the Dead – if you dare.

There's plenty to entertain younger kids too, including a soft play area, more than 170 amusement games, and a Redemption Zone where you can play games to win prizes. There are food outlets but, with The Dubai Mall on your doorstep, it's worth venturing out to explore your dining options.

HIGHLIGHTS
Storm-G
SpinGear
Sonic Hopper

NEARBY ATTRACTIONS
Stay in the mall to visit Dubai Aquarium and Underwater Zoo, or enjoy the views from Burj Khalifa's observation deck, At The Top.

"Brave the thrilling snowboard-style ride, Halfpipe Canyon."

ADVENTURELAND

WHERE Sahara Centre, Level 1
WHEN Daily, 10am until late
Friday, 2pm-midnight
HOW MUCH From Dhs.9.50 per ride
TIME SPENT Half day
CONTACT 06 531 6363
WEBSITE adventureland-sharjah.com
MAP p.218

For days when it's too hot to venture outside, this indoor amusement park at Sahara Centre is a one-stop shop for thrills and spills. Older kids can check out exciting rides such as Quantum Leap, a winding rollercoaster that whizzes up, down and up again to heights of nine metres, and the dizzying Tidal Wave that sends you spinning in huge circles. There's even an indoor log flume ride.

For little ones, there are a number of tamer rides to choose from including the Adventure Train, mini aeroplanes and a carousel. There's also a four-level, Arabian Palace-themed soft play area to keep them entertained.

When you need to catch your breath, head over to the Activity Area for dough sculpting and cake decorating workshops, storytelling, and other more sedate activities.

There are also racing games and simulators, a bowling alley, and the Cliffhanger climbing wall, as well as amusement games and billiards tables. Take a break from all the fun at the Sports Cafe, which serves up kid-friendly snacks, milkshakes and coffees; alternatively, there are plenty of dining options around Sahara Centre. A new two-level go-karting track is set to open in 2014, so watch this space.

HIGHLIGHTS
Tidal Wave
Log Jam
Smasher bumper cars

NEARBY ATTRACTIONS
When the weather is pleasant, wander along the canal at Al Qasba or dine alfresco at Al Majaz Waterfront.

"Check out the Tidal Wave and indoor log flume ride."

MURJAN SPLASH PARK

WHERE Khalifa Park
WHEN Weekdays, 10am-10pm
Weekends, 10am-midnight
HOW MUCH Dhs.10-15 per ride
TIME SPENT Less than three hours
MAP p.208

Located in the vast Khalifa Park, this attraction is the perfect destination for water babies with rides and games aimed at children aged three to 12. The highlight of the park is an enormous waterplay climbing structure with tunnels, water guns and waterslides, and a giant tipping bucket.

There's also a lazy river over 250m long and just 0.6m deep providing more sedate fun – all you have to do is sit back on a tube and relax as the water takes you around the park. Meanwhile the Surf Wrangler, a surfboard simulator, allows mini surfers to test out their balance and surfing skills in a safe environment.

For youngsters that don't fancy making a splash, there's the Lily Pad Hop, a collection of four trampolines. Little ones can jump, flip and bounce with the safety of a harness.

After you've spent a couple of hours enjoying the various attractions – be sure to test out the bumper boats in the Bumper Boat Lagoon for some healthy competition – relax with a picnic in Khalifa Park. The park is one of the largest in Abu Dhabi and a firm favourite with visitors and locals alike, perfect for whiling away the hours during the cooler months. Note that Tuesdays and Wednesdays are for ladies only.

HIGHLIGHTS
Waterplay structure
Lazy river
Bumper Boat Lagoon

NEARBY ATTRACTIONS
Head to Khalifa Park for its picnic spots and play areas, or visit Abu Dhabi Corniche to soak up the sun on the beach.

"Have a friendly fight with friends at the water balloon station."

YAS WATERWORLD

WHERE Yas Island West
WHEN Daily, 10am-8pm
HOW MUCH Dhs.190-435
TIME SPENT Full day
CONTACT 02 414 2000
WEBSITE yaswaterworld.com
MAP p.209

Just when you thought the UAE had all the record-breaking theme parks it could possibly need, along came Yas Waterworld. This gargantuan water park on Yas Island made quite a splash when it burst onto the scene in 2012. You could easily spend an entire day here, trying out the 43 rides, slides and attractions.

Each one is handily categorised into one of four groups: Adrenaline Rush, Exciting Adventure, Moving and Grooving, and Young Fun, and there's something for everyone. For thrill seekers, the Liwa Loop – the first and only waterslide of its kind in the Middle East – is a near-vertical drop that shoots you through a winding loop at an incredible speed. The Dawamma is a 20m-high, heart-pumping twisting funnel that up to six people can enjoy together.

For gentler thrills, try the Sand Viper Strike – a looping slide that is not nearly as frightening as the name suggests – or simply make yourself comfortable on a tube and float down the Al Raha River (lazy river) effortlessly. When you're not enjoying the rides, there are plenty of cafes, restaurants and refreshment stands for refuelling, as well as comfortable sun loungers and cabanas for soaking up some rays.

BEST FOR
Visitors

HIGHLIGHTS
Liwa Loop waterslide
Bandit Bomber rollercoaster
Dawamma group ride

NEARBY ATTRACTIONS
For more adrenaline activities, try a driving experience at Yas Marina Circuit or the record-breaking rollercoaster at Ferrari World.

"Book a cabana and enjoy a personalised food and drinks menu."

AQUAVENTURE

WHERE Atlantis, The Palm
WHEN Daily, 10am. Closing times vary
HOW MUCH Dhs.165 (adults)
Dhs.140 (children)
TIME SPENT Full day
CONTACT 04 426 0000
WEBSITE atlantisthepalm.com
MAP p.213

When it comes to wet and wild thrills in Dubai, there are few places that can compete with Aquaventure. This 42-acre water park is the ultimate destination for family-friendly fun, with enough attractions to keep teens, tots and the young at heart happy.

To get the adrenaline pumping, there's the Leap of Faith, a 27.5m near-vertical drop that shoots you through tunnels surrounded by shark-infested waters. If that's not thrilling enough, the Rapids is a ride on a 1.6km river punctuated by waves and waterfalls. The new Tower of Poseidon boasts heart pumping waterslides plus the Middle East's longest zip line circuit.

Aquaventure is very well-equipped to accommodate mini-adventurers too – Splashers is a giant water playground specifically for little ones. When it's time for a break from the thrill-a-minute rides, you can float down the lazy river or relax and sunbathe on the 700m Aquaventure private beach.

Just as exciting as the rides are the opportunities to get close to sealife. You can wade into Shark Lagoon to hand-feed cow-nosed rays (under the supervision of trained staff), or take a Shark Safari, wearing special breathing equipment that allows you to walk among these predators in their tank.

HIGHLIGHTS
Splashers
Leap of Faith
Shark Safari

NEARBY ATTRACTIONS
At Atlantis, The Palm you can frolic with dolphins in Dolphin Bay, then see even more sealife at The Lost Chambers Aquarium.

"Brave the thrilling Leap of Faith and wade into Shark Lagoon."

WILD WADI WATER PARK

WHERE Jumeirah Beach Hotel
WHEN Daily, 10am. Closing times vary
HOW MUCH Dhs.235 (adults)
Dhs.175 (children under 1.1m)
TIME SPENT Full day
CONTACT 04 348 4444
WEBSITE wildwadi.com
MAP p.213

BEST FOR
Winter

From hurtling down waterslides to lounging on inflatables along a lazy river, there's never a dull moment at Wild Wadi Water Park, home to over 30 rides and attractions. It's the perfect place to spend a sunny afternoon – whether you want to brave the white water rapids or simply bob about in the wave pool. Yes, there can be long queues for some of the big rides, but soak up the sunshine knowing that it will all be worth it for the journey to the bottom.

The highlight is undoubtedly the Jumeirah Sceirah, the tallest and fastest freefall slide outside of the United States. You and a friend climb up a 32m-high tower, step into side-by-side capsules and then the trapdoor floor opens to shoot you down a 120m-long slide at speeds of up to 80kmph. Wipeout and Riptide Flowriders offer the ultimate surfing experience, while at Burj Surj you pile into a tube with a group, admire the view of Dubai's skyline, before being sent into a spin all the way down to the pool.

The water slides and pool activities at Juha's Dhow and Lagoon are a firm family favourite – beware of the dumping bucket though! And Breaker's Bay, the largest pool in the Middle East, provides waves of excitement.

HIGHLIGHTS
Jumeirah Sceirah
Wipeout
Burj Surj

NEARBY ATTRACTIONS
Splash out on a day pass for Dhs.250 at Jumeirah Beach Hotel; sunbathe on the private beach then eat pizza at La Veranda.

"Travel at 80kmph down the Jumeirah Sceirah slide."

ICE LAND WATER PARK

WHERE Al Jazeera, Al Hamra
WHEN Timings vary
HOW MUCH Dhs.150 (adults)
Dhs.100 (children under 1.2m)
TIME SPENT Full day
CONTACT 07 206 7888
WEBSITE icelandwaterpark.com
MAP p.216

The northernmost emirate of Ras Al Khaimah is usually more sought after for its natural beauty rather than its manmade attractions, but Ice Land Water Park is the exception to this rule. With its ice-capped 'mountains' and plastic penguins in the middle of a desert landscape, this gargantuan polar-themed water park is certainly a sight to behold.

Without a doubt, Ice Land is a magnet for tots and toddlers, who can't help but love the quirkiness of it all. There's Kids Cove, with its shallow waters, miniature slides and a sandpit for toddlers, and Penguin Bay, an interactive play area that's home to the UAE's biggest rain dance pool – a pretty impressive 5,600sqm. In keeping with the polar theme, there's also Penguin Falls, one of the tallest manmade waterfalls in the world. Other weird and wonderful attractions include Aqua Games, a regular sized football pitch with soft turf, shallow water and rain showers, and a manmade coral reef complete with fish (real, not plastic) that you can explore by snorkel.

When you're not enjoying the thrill-a-minute rides, there are plenty of spaces to sit, relax and soak up some sun, as well as cafes and restaurants for grabbing a bite to eat.

BEST FOR
Families

HIGHLIGHTS
Kids Cove
Aqua Games
Manmade coral reef

NEARBY ATTRACTIONS
Go horse riding at Banyan Tree Al Wadi then take a dip in the hot springs at Golden Tulip Khatt Springs Resort and Spa.

"Visit Penguin Falls to see the UAE's largest manmade waterfall."

DREAMLAND AQUA PARK

WHERE Nr Barracuda Beach Resort, RAK Highway, Al Rafaah
WHEN Timings vary
HOW MUCH Dhs.135 (adults) Dhs.85 (children)
TIME SPENT Full day
CONTACT 06 768 1888
WEBSITE dreamlanduae.com
MAP p.217

Whether you want to race down daredevil slides or simply dip a toe in the water, there's a great assortment of attractions to enjoy here. Set within lush, landscaped grounds just minutes from the coast, this water park is the perfect getaway from the city.

With more than 30 rides, as well as sporting activities, there's plenty to fill a full day out – whatever your appetite for adventure. For adrenaline junkies, there are freefalling rides such as the Black Hole and the Kamikaze. For younger visitors, or those who enjoy a more leisurely pace, there's a lazy river, a wave pool, and a high-salinity pool for floating about.

Young children can blow off some steam in the Aqua Play area, which has 19 games and attractions. There are also plenty of activities if you'd prefer to stay on dry land: from burning rubber on the 400m go-kart track to spending some time with the furry friends at Mini Pet Land.

Sporty types can hire courts for basketball, beach volleyball or badminton while arcade games and simulators help keep boredom firmly at bay. There's a variety of cafes and restaurants, as well as a licensed pool bar. And, while Dreamland is perfect for a day trip, you can extend your stay and book a tent or cabana hut.

HIGHLIGHTS
Aqua Play
Kamikaze ride
Lazy river

NEARBY ATTRACTIONS
The Barracuda Beach Resort is a pleasant weekend getaway destination that's home to a popular tax-free drinks store.

"Be sure to try the Black Hole, a thrilling freefalling ride."

Thinking hardware? Think again.

There's certainly more to ACE than just a hardware store. From automotive accessories to kitchen appliances, camping gear to barbeques, outdoor furniture to paints and plants, gardening items to pet accessories. There's so much to choose from all under one roof. **ACE. One Store. Many Lifestyles.**

Dubai: Dubai Festival City, Tel: 800 ASK ACE (800 275 223), Sheikh Zayed Road, Tel: (04) 341 1906, Fax: (04) 341 7610 **Abu Dhabi:** Yas Island, Opposite IKEA, Tel: (02) 565 1945, Fax: (02) 565 1836 Mina Road, Tel: (02) 673 1665, Fax: (02) 673 0415, **Sharjah:** Al Wahda Street, Tel: (06) 537 1556, Fax: (06) 537 1575 **Al Ain:** Sultan Bin Zayed Road, Bawadi Mall Tel: (03) 784 0561 **e-mail: ace@alfuttaim.ae or www.al-futtaim.ae**

Beaches
& Parks

ABU DHABI CORNICHE

WHERE Corniche Road West
WHEN Timings vary
HOW MUCH Free entry to public beaches
TIME SPENT Full day
WEBSITE visitabudhabi.ae
MAP p.208

Take one look at the golden stretch of sand along Abu Dhabi's Corniche, and you'll remember why you chose to live in the UAE. This 8km-long waterfront is a great base for a day out and, with its play areas, cafes, gardens and activities, it's a bustling hub for families and friends – particularly during the cooler months from October to May.

Walk, jog, rollerblade or cycle along the wide, paved paths lining the seafront – you can rent bikes along the way – and refuel at one of the many cafes and restaurants (the Hey Sugar cupcake bakery is a particular favourite, if you have a sweet tooth).

There's free parking nearby, and plenty of parks across the road where you can find a shaded spot for an afternoon picnic.

The beaches and beach parks range from those with family access only to public beaches where everyone's welcome. Some are free to enter, while others, such as BAKE beach club, charge a nominal fee for the luxury of a sun lounger with parasol. The beachfront has been awarded Blue Flag status for its clean, safe waters, and is a perfect spot for sandcastle building or sun worshipping. A new 1.5km stretch of pristine white sand has opened on the western side.

HIGHLIGHTS
New 1.5km pristine beach
Beach sports facilities
Waterfront cafes

NEARBY ATTRACTIONS
Visit the iconic Jumeirah at Etihad Towers hotel for excellent dining and stunning panoramic views over the city.

"Rent a bike and cycle from one end of the Corniche to the other."

SAADIYAT PUBLIC BEACH

WHERE Saadiyat Island
WHEN Daily, 8am-6pm
HOW MUCH Prices vary
TIME SPENT Full day
CONTACT 02 115 0848
WEBSITE BAKEuae.com
MAP p.208

Abu Dhabi's pristine beaches and calm, warm waters make it the perfect destination for watersports enthusiasts. One of the best spots for hitting the waves and soaking up the sun is Saadiyat Public Beach, run by BAKE. Visitors can take part in a variety of sports and fitness classes run by Oceanman UAE (oceanmanuae.com) including 'Bake and Shape' stand up paddleboarding sessions. Prices start at Dhs.100, which covers your equipment rental and a briefing on techniques and safety. If you're going with a group of friends, Dhs.200 per person per hour will get you all of that plus a private

one-hour lesson for four people or more and a tour of Saadiyat Island.

The same company also runs kayaking sessions off the beach; more experienced paddlers can simply rent the equipment (Dhs.200 per hour for a single kayak and Dhs.300 per hour for a double) while private lessons and a Saadiyat tour start at Dhs.350 per hour. Once you've had your fill of watersports, Saadiyat Public Beach is the perfect spot to relax and soak up some rays. For a nominal fee, you can rent sun loungers with umbrellas for the day, as well as lockers and towels – beach club-style comfort at a fraction of the price.

BEST FOR
Winter

HIGHLIGHTS
Stand up paddleboarding
Kayaking
Sun loungers for hire

NEARBY ATTRACTIONS
For an indulgent break from a day of watersports and sunbathing, pop into the neighbouring Park Hyatt for lunch.

"Take a tour around Saadiyat by kayak or paddleboard."

AJMAN CORNICHE

WHERE Corniche Avenue
WHEN Timings vary
HOW MUCH Free
TIME SPENT Full day
MAP p.207

The UAE's smallest emirate is also its least developed, and this is what makes Ajman's beachfront so special. There's nothing spoiling the horizon; just palm trees, crystal clear water and golden sands as far as the eye can see. The emirate's coast is a lovely stretch of beach perfect for walking, sunbathing and swimming – and lined with just a few basic amenities.

There's a tidal pool that's free to the public for safe, sheltered swimming, and some fine sandy beaches. By day, the area is relaxed, and several of the shisha bars along the Corniche offer a decent lunch menu – check out Arajeel.

At the southern end, some fast food dining options are scattered along the beachfront, while further north there are some great restaurants on the other side of the road. Try Themar Al Bahar, which serves up mountains of fresh seafood, or Attibrah, which has some tasty traditional Emirati dishes and delicious mezze on the menu.

There are amusements all along the promenade, and watersports are available at the larger hotels to the northern end of the Corniche. Visit the Kempinski Hotel Ajman, where you can try your hand at activities like windsurfing and kayaking.

HIGHLIGHTS
Tidal pool
Uninterrupted views
Watersports

NEARBY ATTRACTIONS
Learn about the emirate's history at Ajman Museum or book a horse riding lesson at the Ajman Equestrian Club.

"Be sure to factor in time to dine on the delicious mezze at Attibrah."

JBR BEACH

WHERE Near The Walk, Jumeirah Beach Residence
HOW MUCH Free
TIME SPENT Full day
MAP p.213

There aren't many public beaches in Dubai within walking distance of shops and cafes – and the Jumeirah Beach Residence (JBR) Beach is by far the best. Brave the busy Dubai Marina traffic and you'll be rewarded with a 2km stretch of golden sand and warm, shallow waters. Yes, there is some ongoing construction, but you can still put that behind you and enjoy the sand and sea.

The areas in front of the hotels are for guests only, but there's plenty of beach in between (from the Sheraton Jumeirah to Le Royal Meridien). Head for the car park at the Hilton end of The Walk, then claim a patch of sand and enjoy a day by the sea.

The waters are fairly calm and the shallow areas are scattered with bathers from dusk 'til dawn, while the hotels offer a variety of watersports such as wakeboarding and banana boating. Or, you could sign up for a camel ride. It's by far one of the most fun, family-friendly beaches in Dubai, and the skyscrapers of Dubai Marina provide a spectacular backdrop.

After a day on the sand, soak up the cosmopolitan atmosphere of The Walk with a stroll along this bustling cobbled promenade, taking in the arts and crafts stalls and ad hoc street entertainment, and stopping for an iced coffee at Zaatar W Zeit.

HIGHLIGHTS
Sun loungers for hire
Watersports

NEARBY ATTRACTIONS
If you fancy heading indoors, Marina Mall is packed with shops, restaurants, a cinema, and Favourite Things play centre.

"Have a camel ride on the beach – and don't forget the camera!"

JUMEIRAH BEACH PARK

WHERE Jumeira Rd, Jumeira 2
WHEN Sunday to Wednesday,
8am-10pm. Thursday to Saturday and
holidays, 8am-11pm
Monday (ladies only)
HOW MUCH Dhs.5 or Dhs.20 per car
TIME SPENT Full day
MAP p.214

You really get the best of both worlds when you visit Jumeirah Beach Park: plenty of grassy areas as well as vast expanses of beach. The entrance fee is a bargain at Dhs.5 per person, or Dhs.20 per car, including all occupants, and for this minimal price you get the run of a pristine, palm-lined beach with clear blue waters that are perfectly safe for swimming.

The facilities include sunbed and parasol hire to help you keep cool – these cost Dhs.20 but get there early to ensure they haven't run out. There are also lifeguards on duty, toilets, showers, and a budget-friendly beachfront snack bar.

Away from the beach, the grassy areas and landscaped gardens are great for setting up picnics or getting a group of friends together for a game of cricket, football or frisbee. There are children's play areas and barbecue pits available for public use, making it a great spot for family beach trips.

During the cooler months, it's worth venturing onto Jumeira Road for a stroll. There's a laidback holiday vibe to the road that any visitor will certainly appreciate, and a wealth of dining options – check out the Lebanese cafe Shu for some post-beach shisha, or the atmospheric Samad Al Iraqi for lunch.

BEST FOR WInter

HIGHLIGHTS
Beachfront snack bar
Kids play area
BBQ pits

NEARBY ATTRACTIONS
Jumeirah Mosque is easily reached from Jumeirah Beach Park, and is the only one in Dubai open to non-Muslim visitors.

"Get there at 8am when it's cool, and have a picnic on the sand."

KITESURFERS' BEACH

WHERE Nr Dubai Offshore Sailing Club, off Jumeira Road, Umm Suqeim
HOW MUCH Free
TIME SPENT Full day
MAP p.214

If you're after an activity-fuelled day by the sea then Kitesurfers' Beach – also known as Kite Beach or Wollongong Beach – is the one for you. Dubai's sportiest beach is by far its coolest, and a firm favourite with local kitesurfers – the long sweeping stretch of uninterrupted sand allows for good waves and makes it the perfect playground for this adrenaline-pumping activity. If you prefer to stay on dry land it's also a great, and often windy, spot for flying a kite.

The beach is a hub for other sports both in and out of the water – check out The Shack (056 693 9258), a beach gym that offers a fitness experience with a difference. You can either pay a Dhs.45 drop-in fee to use the facilities, or sign up for one of their fitness classes to enjoy a workout session with a gorgeous beach view.

There are affordable kayaks for hire, a play area, beach volleyball and soap soccer court, as well as showers and toilets. A small shop serves drinks and there are plenty of cafes along Jumeira Road for snacks. Your best bet is to pick up some yummy fish and chips from Rock 'n' Sole Plaice at the Park'n Shop complex on Al Wasl Road, and then enjoy them on the beach while you watch the kitesurfers in action.

HIGHLIGHTS
Kayaks for hire
Kitesurfing
Beach gym

NEARBY ATTRACTIONS
The neighbouring public Umm Suqeim Beach is known for its stunning backdrop of the Burj Al Arab, a perfect spot for visitors.

"Plan a later visit and go kayaking as the sun sets over the sea."

MAMZAR BEACH PARK

WHERE Al Khaleej Rd, Al Mamzar
WHEN Sunday to Wednesday
8am-10pm. Thursday to Saturday
8am-11pm. Mondays are ladies only
HOW MUCH Dhs.5 or Dhs.30 per car
TIME SPENT Full day
MAP p.215

There's more to Mamzar Beach Park than getting your toes in the sand – much more. With its four clean beaches, green, open spaces, private chalets and imaginative play areas, this is a park and a half. What's more, it's usually quite pleasantly empty during the week.

The well-maintained beaches have sheltered, safe areas for swimming and, away from the ocean, there are two swimming pools with areas for both kids and adults. Changing rooms with showers, parasols and lifeguards all add to the beach club experience.

To help you make the most out of your day, you can rent an air-conditioned chalet with barbecue from Dhs.150, or simply take your pick of one of the modern barbecue areas with umbrellas and seats. There's also a restaurant as well as several snack bars scattered around the park.

There are plenty of activities in Mamzar Beach Park to keep visitors of all ages entertained: adults can hire bikes, jet skis and other equipment and kids have the run of play areas and climbing obstacles. Further along from the beach park, there are beaches on the lagoon that are free to use – providing more space for sunbathing. You can also try flyboarding, the latest watersports craze.

BEST FOR Families

HIGHLIGHTS
Two swimming pools
Private chalets
Play areas

NEARBY ATTRACTIONS
Pop across the border to Sharjah and visit the Sharjah Aquarium. Your ticket includes entry to the Sharjah Maritime Museum.

"Hire an air-conditioned chalet with a barbecue for the day."

UMM SUQEIM BEACH

WHERE Near Jumeirah Beach Hotel, Jumeira Road
HOW MUCH Free
TIME SPENT Full day
MAP p.214

This lovely stretch of sand, also known as Sunset Beach or Surfers' Beach, is one of the busiest public beaches at weekends, especially Fridays. It's also on the Dubai Big Bus Tour route. The white sands extend all the way from Jumeirah Beach Hotel to Kitesurfers' Beach.

The beach's prime spot next to the Burj Al Arab allows for some stunning backdrop photos, hence its popularity, and makes it a winner for impressing visitors. Head here mid-week to enjoy the golden sands and relatively clear waters without the crowds. New lifeguard centres will soon open at intervals along the beach and, while there are no toilet facilities at present, there are several petrol stations nearby if nature calls. For snacks, there's a ladies-only cafe in the park opposite, plus plenty of options on Jumeira Road for picking up a picnic .

While Dubai isn't known as a surfing destination, you will find an enthusiastic community of surfers who are out whenever there's a swell, as the beach gets smallish but decent waves; surfing season in Dubai is between October and April. Umm Suqeim Beach is also popular with stand up paddleboarders; strut around with a board under your arm and you'll fit right in.

BEST FOR
Visitors

HIGHLIGHTS
Surfing
Stand up paddleboarding
Cafes on Jumeira Road

NEARBY ATTRACTIONS
Brave the waterslides at Wild Wadi Water Park, then head to Souk Madinat Jumeirah to shop for trinkets and souvenirs.

"Take great holiday snapshots with the Burj Al Arab as a backdrop."

FAMILY PARK

WHERE Al Khaleej Al Arabi St
WHEN Weekdays, 8am-10pm
Weekends, 8am-11pm
HOW MUCH Dhs.1
TIME SPENT Full day
MAP p.208

One of the best things about Abu Dhabi is that, despite being the UAE capital, this bustling city is full of gorgeous green spaces for relaxing and socialising. Perhaps the most popular is Family Park, a firm favourite with parents and children alike with themed play areas, tree-lined walkways for strolling, jogging and cycling, and shaded lawns for afternoon picnics.

Located just a few minutes' walk from the beach and Corniche, Family Park has a number of play zones to keep the young ones entertained, including a toddler village with a toy train and fire engine, and a pirate ship.

You'll also find swings, slides, climbing frames and tunnels in a variety of sandy playgrounds.

Among the walkways, fountains and landscaped gardens, there are plenty of picnic spots. There's a central cafe serving light refreshments throughout the day, or you can pick up supplies at the Abu Dhabi Cooperative Society on the south side of the park.

Although the park is best enjoyed during the cooler months, it really comes alive during the Let's Go Summer festivals in June and July. During this time, there's a wide range of activities and games to enjoy, from soap soccer to waterslides.

HIGHLIGHTS
Toddler play areas
Picnic spots
Football play area

NEARBY ATTRACTIONS
The skate park next door has plenty of ramps, twists and turns where daring teens can show off their skills.

"Bring your bike and explore the tree-lined walkways on wheels."

AL AIN OASIS

WHERE Off Zayed Ibn Sultan St
WHEN Timings vary
HOW MUCH Free
TIME SPENT Less than three hours
MAP p.210

This impressive oasis in the heart of Al Ain – which is also known as the Oasis City – is filled with palm plantations, many of which are still working farms. The largest oasis in the city, there are more than 145,000 date palms under cultivation here and the spot is believed to have been used for this practice for some 3,000 years.

There are eight different entrances to Al Ain Oasis, some of which have arched gates, and there is no entry fee. You could drive your car through the tight network of paved roads and pathways, but getting on your bike or exploring on foot allows you to take in the scenery.

The cool, shady walkways transport you from the heat and noise of the city to an otherworldly, tranquil haven. While you are welcome to wander through the plantations, it's best to stick to the paved areas.

The farms provide a fascinating insight into the history of the area, as many of them still have working examples of falaj, the traditional irrigation system that has been used for centuries to tap into underground wells. If you're lucky, you might stumble across some distinctive traditional farm properties or even farmers gathering a harvest, depending on the time of year.

HIGHLIGHTS
Date plantations
Shaded walkways
Traditional wells

NEARBY ATTRACTIONS
To learn even more about UAE history, wander around the displays at Al Ain Palace Museum or Al Ain National Museum.

"Keep an eye out for the traditional irrigation systems known as falaj."

AL JAHILI PARK

WHERE Zayed Bin Sultan St
WHEN 5am-1am
HOW MUCH Free
TIME SPENT Less than three hours
WEBSITE visitabudhabi.ae
MAP p.210

With a nickname like 'the Garden City', it's no wonder that Al Ain is blessed with so many open green spaces. The main park – and most popular – in the area is Al Jahili Park, also known to some as Al Ain Public Gardens.

Located on Zayed Bin Sultan Street, this popular, picturesque park provides a welcome leafy area where friends and family congregate at the weekends and in the evenings during the cooler months. There's a wide variety of play equipment to entertain the little ones in the playground, and there are a few amusement arcade games for older children to keep boredom at bay.

Time your visit for the end of the day to see the fountains all lit up – it's very atmospheric for a walk.

Another pleasant spot to while away an afternoon is Al Ain Ladies Park, located off Zayed Al Awwal Street. Also known as Basra Park, this is a tranquil green space that's reserved for women and children only (boys must be aged 10 or under). It's a popular hangout throughout the week with mums and kids.

There are plenty of shaded seating areas to set up camp while the children run off and play, and there's a small cafe where you can pick up a bite to eat.

BEST FOR
Families

HIGHLIGHTS
Shaded seating
Adventure playground
Amusement arcade games

NEARBY ATTRACTIONS
For a more active afternoon, try the watersports at Wadi Adventure or check out the theme park rides at Hili Fun City.

"Stay in the park to see the fountains lit up in the evening."

CREEK PARK

WHERE Nr Al Garhoud Bridge
WHEN Sunday to Wednesday,
8am-10pm. Thursday to Saturday and
holidays, 8am-11pm
HOW MUCH Dhs.5
TIME SPENT Full day
MAP p.215

Situated in the heart of the city but blessed with acres of gardens, fishing piers, jogging tracks, barbecue sites, children's play areas, mini-golf, restaurants and kiosks, this is the ultimate in Middle Eastern park life. Creek Park sits on the bank of Dubai Creek opposite the striking sail-shaped building of the Dubai Creek Golf & Yacht Club.

To get a bird's eye view of the park, the creek and Old Dubai, take a trip in a cable car – a scenic half hour ride that runs the 2.3km stretch of the park. And for the kids, or anyone without a head for heights, there's a miniature train departing from

Gate 1. The area feels worlds away from the futuristic charms of New Dubai. Instead, this park focuses on more traditional attractions: there's a mini falaj system of canals, a desert garden and a large amphitheatre, as well as camel and pony rides available near Gate 1.

From Gates 1 and 4, you and your friends can hire four-wheel cycles for Dhs.30 per hour. You can't use your own bike in the park, although rollerblading is permitted. This spacious park is also home to Dubai Dolphinarium and Children's City, both of which are worth a visit – if you can find the time.

HIGHLIGHTS
Cable car
Dubai Dolphinarium
Children's City

NEARBY ATTRACTIONS
Al Fahidi Historical Neighbourhood (formerly known as Bastakiya) boasts some great galleries and museums.

"Brave the heights to enjoy stunning views from the cable car."

MIRACLE GARDEN

WHERE Shk Mohammed Bin Zayed Rd,
Nr Arabian Ranches
WHEN Timings vary
HOW MUCH Dhs.20
TIME SPENT Less than three hours
CONTACT 04 422 8902
WEBSITE dubaimiraclegarden.com
MAP p.213

In a city that boasts many of the world's most iconic architectural structures, a visit to the explosion of colour that is Miracle Garden provides a wonderful respite from the skyscraper valleys. Miracle Garden has been developed with the vision of becoming the world's biggest flower garden – no mean feat in the arid climate of Dubai.

It's perfect for an afternoon stroll – you can walk under flower-covered arches and romantic blooms fashioned into the shapes of hearts and stars. It's a fun place to chill out with the family, and a romantic venue to relax on picnic benches surrounded by the region's unique flora.

The sheer volume of blooms on display in the park is astonishing. It's estimated that there are more than 45 million flowers for visitors to admire, comprised of around 45 different species. What's more, the garden holds the Guinness World Record for the world's longest wall of flowers – be sure to check that out during your visit.

There are plans to add even more features including a children's play area. Most recently, a brand new butterfly garden has opened up in the heart of the park – a huge structure comprising nine domes filled with these brightly coloured creatures.

HIGHLIGHTS
More than 45 million blooms
Butterfly garden
Wall of flowers

NEARBY ATTRACTIONS
Miracle Garden is a short drive from Dubai Autodrome, where visitors of all ages can try karting on the indoor and outdoor tracks.

"Escape the sun and visit
the indoor domes in the
butterfly garden."

MUSHRIF PARK

WHERE Al Khawaneej Rd, Mushrif
WHEN Sunday to Wednesday, 8am-10pm. Thursday to Saturday and holidays, 8am-11pm
HOW MUCH Dhs.3 per person or Dhs.10 per car
TIME SPENT Full day
MAP p.215

This desert-like park near Mirdif is full of surprises. If you head to Mushrif Park, you'll be rewarded with play areas, a 5km walking, cycling and jogging track, two 25-metre swimming pools (entry to the swimming pool is Dhs.10 for adults and Dhs.5 for children), an equestrian centre, a fun fair with trampolines, and even a miniature village.

The park is so vast that you can even drive through it, and it's somewhat satisfying to discover such a wide open space well away from the skyscrapers of Dubai. This natural attraction feels a world away from the busy city. Mushrif Park is also a great place to spend an afternoon if you're a nature lover. There's a petting zoo and aviary, as well as an animal enclosure with camels, goats and horses; you may even spot the odd peacock strutting about the park.

If you're interested in horses be sure to check out the Mushrif Equestrian and Polo Club – definitely one of the highlights of the park. Riders of all ages and abilities are welcome to try their hand at this traditional Emirati pastime; lessons are available to polish up your skills, and there are guided rides across the desert terrain. The club even organises moonlit rides across the terrain.

HIGHLIGHTS
Swimming pool
Petting zoo
Equestrian club

NEARBY ATTRACTIONS
After an afternoon in the park, visit Mirdif City Centre; head for the cinema or make a splash on Aquaplay's indoor log flume.

"Book a lesson with the Mushrif Equestrian and Polo Club."

SAFA PARK

WHERE Nr Union Co-op, Al Wasl Rd
WHEN Sunday to Wednesday,
8am-10pm. Thursday to Saturday,
8am-11pm
HOW MUCH Dhs.3
TIME SPENT Full day
MAP p.214

This huge artistically landscaped park is a great place to escape the commotion of nearby Sheikh Zayed Road. Its sports fields, barbecue areas and play areas make it one of the best parks in the city.

There's lots to entertain the kids, including a boating lake in the centre and a small maze, and plenty of paths that are perfect for wobbly toddlers on bikes with stabilisers. Tennis and basketball courts are free to use, and head there on any weekend or evening to find informal football and cricket games playing out on the large grassy areas. There's a great community feel to this park: private birthday parties in secluded corners, charity events, and a flea market on the first Saturday of every month during the winter (dubai-fleamarket.com). Every Friday morning there's the seasonal Ripe Foodie Friday Market (ripeme.com) near Gate 5 featuring a brilliant range of produce, arts and crafts.

The Archive arts library and cafe (thearchive.ae) makes for a welcome pit stop, especially for breakfast, and there's a Union Co-op and a Choithrams opposite the park where you can pick up supplies for a picnic. Nearby BookMunch cafe has a takeaway lunch hamper – be sure to sample their legendary carrot cake.

HIGHLIGHTS
Seasonal markets
Boating lake
Running track

NEARBY ATTRACTIONS
Wasl Square is perfect for a spot of retail therapy. Round off your day by having pizza for dinner at The Pantry.

"Visit The Archive for breakfast and browse its library."

ZABEEL PARK

WHERE Sheikh Zayed Road, Nr Trade Centre roundabout
WHEN Sunday to Wednesday, 8.30am-10pm. Thursday to Saturday, 8am-11pm
HOW MUCH Dhs.5
TIME SPENT Full day
MAP p.215

This green oasis straddles Sheikh Zayed Road in the shadow of Trade Centre roundabout – but you wouldn't even know it from the inside. The landscaping and facilities here are superb: winding, tree-lined walkways, unusual sculptures (from a kangaroo to a Chinese house) and activities around every corner.

The northern half of the park is home to a wonderfully fun and well-shaded children's adventure play area, with all kinds of ropes and obstacles to climb, and some funky slides that are very popular with little ones. There's also a large amphitheatre and a football pitch. Once you cross the pedestrian bridge over the highway (or you can catch the mini train), you can explore the other section of the park, which has a beautifully serene lake with little rock pools feeding off from it. There are motorised boats available for hire for Dhs.5. From this part of the park, you can get a great snapshot of the skyline of SZR, but feel strangely far away from it.

Dotted throughout are cafes and kiosks for grabbing a bite to eat, as well as picnic and barbecue areas, and toilets. There's also a running track around the exterior, and some exercise equipment to try out if you're feeling active.

HIGHLIGHTS
Boat hire
Cricket and football pitch
Adventure play areas

NEARBY ATTRACTIONS
After your trip to the park, be sure to visit nearby Karama for lunch or dinner, and enjoy some delicious Indian cuisine.

"Rent a two or four-seater bike and explore the park on wheels."

Open doors. Open minds.

Sheikh Mohammed bin Rashid Centre
for Cultural Understanding

الأبْواب مفتوحة. العقول متفتحة.

مركز الشيخ محمد بن راشد آل مكتوم
للتواصل الحضاري

The SMCCU strives to remove barriers between people of different nationalities and raise awareness of the UAE's local culture, customs and religion. Located in a traditional wind tower house in the heart of Al Fahidi Historic District, the SMCCU regularly conducts various activities that aim to improve cross- cultural understanding and communication between locals and guests across the UAE.

Jumeirah Mosque Visit

The Jumeirah Mosque has become renowned as the focal point of SMCCU's **"Open doors. Open minds."** programme. Till recently, it was the only mosque in Dubai open to the public and dedicated to receiving non-Muslim guests.
Every Saturday through Thursday at 10am. (closed Friday).
Modest dress is preferred; traditional attire can also be borrowed from the mosque. AED 10 pp.
Duration 75 mins (No reservations required).

Cultural Meals

The most popular offering of the SMCCU is its Cultural Breakfasts & Lunches. Introduced for 2013 is our new Brunch & Dinner events where guests can also indulge in traditional Emirati meals in a relaxed and friendly ambience while a knowledgeable Emirati host chats to them about the local customs and traditions.
Breakfast: Every Mon & Wed at 10am, AED 60 pp.
Lunch: Every Sunday & Tuesday at 1pm, AED 70 pp.
Brunch: Every Saturday at 10:30am, AED 80 pp.
Dinner: Every Tuesday at 7pm, AED 95 pp.
Duration 90 minutes, (Reservations are essential).

Walking Tour & Heritage Tour

Enjoy a guided walk through the Al Fahidi Historic District followed by a Question & Answer session at the SMCCU house with freshly brewed Arabic coffee and dates. Heritage Tour includes a visit and talk inside the Diwan Masjid (Mosque).
Walking Tour: Sunday through Thursday at 9am, AED 35 pp
Heritage Tour: Saturday at 9am & every Sunday, Tuesday and Thursday at 10:30am, AED 55 pp.
Duration 60 minutes Walking Tour, 90 minutes Heritage Tour,
(Reservations are essential).

To find out more and book online, visit us at www.cultures.ae or call 9714 353-6666
@SMCCUDubai

Sights & Attractions

MANARAT AL SAADIYAT

WHERE Saadiyat Island
WHEN Daily, 9am-8pm
HOW MUCH Free
TIME SPENT Full day
CONTACT 02 657 5800
WEBSITE saadiyatculturaldistrict.ae
MAP p.208

BEST FOR
Summer

Saadiyat Cultural District on Abu Dhabi's Saadiyat Island is a fabulous cultural development that, in the coming years, will be home to some truly world-class museums housed in soon-to-be iconic buildings – including the Louvre Abu Dhabi in 2015, designed by Jean Nouvel, and the Guggenheim Abu Dhabi to follow that in 2017, designed by Frank Gehry.

However, for a dose of culture there's no need to wait – head for Manarat Al Saadiyat, a wonderful exhibition space with several galleries (and a superb restaurant, Fanr) that are well worth a visit. Meaning the 'place of enlightenment', Manarat Al

Saadiyat has three galleries hosting temporary exhibitions. In the past these have included works by Picasso, Klee, Bacon and other masters. There are also interactive exhibitions aimed at children of all ages, which will keep the whole family entertained.

The centre hosts regular discussion platforms throughout the year, as well as workshops for adults and children in a designated art room. A permanent gallery entitled The Saadiyat Story is a stunning space with models, maps and enormous screens, which shows how Saadiyat Island is rapidly transforming, and its ambitious plans for the future as a cultural hub of the UAE.

HIGHLIGHTS
Guided tours
Art galleries
Family-friendly workshops

NEARBY ATTRACTIONS
Dine at Fanr, a bright, arty cafe with a passionate approach to food that also sells gourmet ingredients to take home and cook.

"Check out the Saadiyat Story, which details the island's development."

AL FAHIDI HISTORICAL NEIGHBOURHOOD

WHERE Nr Al Seef Rd, Al Souk Al Kabeer
WHEN Timings vary
HOW MUCH Prices vary
TIME SPENT Full day
CONTACT 04 353 9090
WEBSITE dubaiculture.ae
MAP p.215

Escape the skyscraper valleys of the city and travel back in time with a trip to Al Fahidi Historical Neighbourhood. Formerly known as Bastakiya, this atmospheric area in Bur Dubai is one of the oldest heritage sites in the city, with a neighbourhood that dates back to the early 1900s.

A wander around offers a beguiling glimpse into a bygone era, with traditional windtowers, bustling courtyards and a maze of winding alleyways. There are some great cultural attractions to visit in the area, including the Dubai Museum. Located in Al Fahidi Fort, this family-friendly attraction showcases all aspects of

BEST FOR History

traditional Emirati life, from souks and oases to archaeological finds and local wildlife. Afterwards, head for the art galleries. The Majlis Gallery is a restored traditional house with a variety of contemporary art – XVA Gallery is a hip hangout that boasts a boutique hotel.

Take a stroll along the creek to the hustle and bustle of the textile souk. You can head for the abra station and take a trip along Dubai Creek. Or, cross the water to explore Shindagha, another interesting historical area where you'll find Sheikh Saeed Al Maktoum House and the Heritage and Diving Villages.

HIGHLIGHTS
XVA Gallery
Dubai Museum
The Majlis Gallery

NEARBY ATTRACTIONS
Grab lunch at XVA Cafe, an excellent vegetarian eatery in XVA Gallery and one of Dubai's best kept secrets.

"Ride an abra on the creek from Maktoum Bridge to Shindagha."

ALSERKAL AVENUE

WHERE Street 8, Al Quoz Industrial 1
WHEN Timings vary
HOW MUCH Prices vary
TIME SPENT Full day
CONTACT 04 416 1900
WEBSITE alserkalavenue.ae
MAP p.214

The rather dusty industrial area that is Al Quoz doesn't usually make it onto most visitors' itineraries but there's more to the neighbourhood than meets the eye. In fact, it's home to one of the most vibrant art scenes in the UAE, with a myriad of galleries and interesting design shops tucked away in hidden warehouses, all just waiting to be discovered.

At the heart of this burgeoning scene is Alserkal Avenue, an extensive arts district that's home to around 20 creative spaces. Some of the area's most amazing exhibition spaces are housed practically back-to-back, making them easy to explore, and they are great places to spot new talent from the UAE and abroad. There's Salsali Private Museum, a non-profit museum, and hip gallery Mojo, both of which are known for championing local artists. Gulf Photo Plus is a photography studio and gallery that runs courses as well as exhibitions. There's also the Third Line, which is known for its innovative displays. Meanwhile, The Fridge has become something of a hidden gem for performance art and music events.

The neighbourhood can be tricky to navigate, and the easiest way to explore Alserkal Avenue is with the aid of ArtMap (see artinthecity.com).

HIGHLIGHTS
The Fridge
The Third Line
Salsali Private Museum

NEARBY ATTRACTIONS
Admire the treasures at the Dubai Antique Museum and the traditional artwork and handicrafts at Total Arts.

"Visit The Fridge for live music from local and international artists."

SHARJAH ART MUSEUM

WHERE Sharjah Arts Area
WHEN Saturday to Thursday,
8am-8pm. Friday, 4pm-8pm
HOW MUCH Free
TIME SPENT Less than three hours
CONTACT 06 568 8222
WEBSITE sharjahmuseums.ae
MAP p.218

Sharjah's museums really take the crown when it comes to cultural highlights of the UAE, and Sharjah's art scene is wonderfully diverse and energetic. Its status as one of the most important in the region is compounded by the Sharjah Biennial, which brings artists together from all over the world.

Sharjah Art Museum holds some superb exhibitions throughout the year, including a brilliant permanent Orientalists exhibition from the personal collection of Sheikh Dr Sultan bin Mohammad Al Qasimi, Ruler of Sharjah. The collection includes lithographs depicting traditional Arab life from the perspective of several preeminent European artists.

A number of contemporary exhibitions are often held here, as well as within the growing number of surrounding buildings. Internationally renowned artists such as Lara Favaretto have held exhibitions in the old, traditional buildings, which make for fantastically atmospheric and unique spaces. Be sure to check out Bait Al Serkal and Bait Al Shamsi, as well as the newly developed spaces in Sharjah Heritage Area for further exhibitions. Back in the museum's main building, there's a fine art reference library, bookshop and cafe.

HIGHLIGHTS
Orientalists collection
Well-stocked bookshop

NEARBY ATTRACTIONS
Once you've finished exploring the arts area, the souks and courtyards of Sharjah Heritage Area are also worth a visit.

"Visit Bait Al Serkal, a restored 19th century building and arts venue."

SPARKY'S FAMILY FUN PARK

WHERE Mushrif Mall
WHEN Weekdays, 9am-midnight
Weekends, 10am-midnight
HOW MUCH Prices start at Dhs.115
TIME SPENT Less than three hours
CONTACT 02 491 4445
WEBSITE sparkys.info
MAP p.208

One of the newest family fun centres in Abu Dhabi, Sparky's is already a firm favourite with the city's residents. Located in Mushrif Mall, it's the perfect treat for little ones after an afternoon of shopping.

Sparky's boasts a wide range of attractions to keep even the most energetic of kids entertained. There is a handful of funfair-style rides, the highlight of which has to be the rollercoaster, although the bumper cars are a close second. Sporty types will love the football striker zone and bowling alley, while for (slightly) more sedate entertainment, there are state-of-the-art arcade games to keep

both tots and teens happy. A 3D and 4D cinema provides some exhilarating entertainment for everyone and a welcome break from the rides.

For a cool indoor activity during the hot summer months, there's also an ice rink where visitors can lace up their skates for a relaxed skating lesson or even have a go at winter sports such as ice hockey and curling. The activity centre can be hired out for various birthday packages.

Visitors to Sparky's purchase Play Cards and load them with credit. Prices start at Dhs.115, which includes Dhs.35 to spend on the games and rides of your choice.

HIGHLIGHTS
4D cinema
Rollercoaster
Bumper cars

NEARBY ATTRACTIONS
After spending some time at Sparky's, have a relaxing browse around the mall or grab a sweet treat at Bloomsbury Cupcakes.

"Get behind the wheel at the funfair-style bumper cars."

WANASA LAND

WHERE Al Wahda Mall
WHEN Timings vary
HOW MUCH Prices start from Dhs.5
TIME SPENT Full day
CONTACT 02 443 7654
WEBSITE alwahda-mall.com
MAP p.208

This entertainment centre at Al Wahda Mall in the heart of Abu Dhabi (next to Al Nahyan Stadium) is a great destination for the whole family, with lots of attractions to choose from. For younger children, there's a large soft play area and animal-themed carousels and amusement rides, as well as fun activities like face painting to keep them entertained.

The miniature village called Wanoos Village boasts a kid-sized cinema, bakery and bookshop – great for toddlers. Older children have their choice of dozens of high-tech computerised games, as well as an electronic shooting range and several hair-raising funfair rides. There's even a climbing wall, as well as bumper cars and billiards tables. The whole family can enjoy Wanasa Land's bowling lanes, and the popular indoor paintball centre is guaranteed to bring out your competitive streak.

The food court is right next door and has lots of restaurants and fast food outlets – both the usual mall suspects and some more interesting options. When your family has had their fill of Wanasa Land, there's also a nine-screen cinema at Al Wahda Mall as well as a good range of shops – both big international chains and local favourites.

HIGHLIGHTS
Miniature Wanoos Village
Climbing wall
Paintballing centre

NEARBY ATTRACTIONS
Once you've enjoyed all the entertainment Al Wahda Mall has to offer, head to Abu Dhabi Corniche to soak up some sun.

"Gather a team together to enjoy some indoor paintballing."

AQUAPLAY

WHERE Mirdif City Centre
WHEN Weekdays, 10am-10pm
Weekends, 10am-midnight
HOW MUCH From Dhs.10
TIME SPENT Less than three hours
CONTACT 04 2316307
WEBSITE theplaymania.com
MAP p.215

Finding a water park where you don't need swimsuits and sun cream is like finding a hidden gem for parents during the summer months – that and the fact that you won't get wet – well, not that much! While Aquaplay is more of an indoor play centre that's dedicated to water fun, kids will love it just the same.

Perfect for two to eight year olds, Aquaplay features a variety of interactive, educational games and water rides. There are arcade-style amusement games with an aqua twist, as well as an experimentation 'lab' with water guns, a swinging pirate ship, a seahorse carousel, and a more

boisterous bumper boat ride that's fun for mums and dads too.

The 'stand and play' activity area with miniature boats, canals, water jets and waterwheels, is a hit for kids who love to splash about – be sure to dress them in the plastic overalls provided as they *will* get wet! The highlight of any visit though is the tot-sized log flume ride. Finish with a trip to Pelican Bay, the fishing port-themed soft play area that's like Dr Who's Tardis inside.

Tucked away at the end of Mirdif City Centre, this is a child-friendly change from the outdoor water parks – and a lot cheaper too, with rides costing between Dhs.10 and Dhs.35.

HIGHLIGHTS
Swinging pirate ship
Log flume ride
Pelican Bay soft play area

NEARBY ATTRACTIONS
Mirdif City Centre is full of family-friendly attractions including Magic Planet, Little Explorers and iFLY Dubai.

"Be sure to check out the boisterous bumper boat rides."

CHILDREN'S CITY

WHERE Creek Park, Gate 1
WHEN Saturday to Thursday,
9am-8.30pm. Friday, 3pm-8.30pm
HOW MUCH Prices start at Dhs.10
TIME SPENT Full day
CONTACT 04 334 0808
WEBSITE childrencity.ae
MAP p.215

For a family-friendly day out that's as fun as it is educational, head for Children's City. This themed activity centre in Creek Park is the first of its kind and offers kids their own learning zone and amusement facilities. It's designed to complement what they've been learning at school, with interactive, hands-on displays to keep things interesting.

A planetarium focuses on the solar system and space exploration, a nature centre provides all the information children could ever need on the world around them and beneath the waves, and the Discovery Space explores the miracles and mysteries of the human body. Another highlight is the International Centre, where children can learn about how their peers in other countries live.

The best thing about Children's City is that there's something to suit everyone; while the exhibition space is aimed at visitors aged five to 15, toddlers and older teens are also well catered for, and the young at heart are sure to enjoy this day out too.

During special holidays such as Eid, the edutainment venue hosts a range of activities. Plus, in addition to the permanent attractions, there are regular events such as light displays and drumming shows.

HIGHLIGHTS
Discovery Space
Nature centre
Light displays and drumming shows

NEARBY ATTRACTIONS
Visit the Dubai Dolphinarium, where you can swim with dolphins or see the UAE's biggest exotic bird show.

"Don't miss the Discovery Space and the planetarium."

KIDS CONNECTION

WHERE Wafi Mall
WHEN Weekdays, 10am-10pm.
Weekends, 10am-midnight
HOW MUCH Prices start from Dhs.3
TIME SPENT Full day
CONTACT 04 327 9011
WEBSITE wafi.com
MAP p.215

While the UAE boasts some brilliant parks, the sweltering summer temperatures means that the majority of them can't be enjoyed all year round. Fortunately, for those days when you want a playground park experience but it's too hot to be outside, there's Kids Connection.

Located on the first floor of Wafi Mall, this bright, colourful – and dazzlingly new – attraction brings the outside in with a variety of wooden park attractions in a very green, woodland-inspired setting. Kids can climb, swing, seesaw and slide while mum and dad enjoy a coffee in the Cafe Court – or burn off some energy on the trampolines, bouncy castle and climbing wall. The soft play area with ball pool is great for toddlers too.

There's a private birthday party room for hire, but when it's not in use kids have free run of the 'virtual' party games – from air hockey to noughts and crosses. The staff here are particularly friendly and add to the fun atmosphere with impromptu games of tag and musical chairs.

Prices range from Dhs.3 to Dhs.27. There are also a few small rides in the cafe area, costing Dhs.2 a go – and an ice cream stall to round off a perfect outing. All in all, a fun play area that's a breath of fresh air for parents!

HIGHLIGHTS
Wooden caterpillar seesaw
Bouncy castle
Trampolines

NEARBY ATTRACTIONS
If you're still in the mood for fun and games, round off your afternoon with glow-in-the-dark mini golf at Tee & Putt.

"The wooden climbing frame brings the outdoors in."

KIDZANIA

WHERE The Dubai Mall, Level 2
WHEN Timings vary
HOW MUCH From Dhs.140
TIME SPENT Full day
CONTACT 04 448 5222
WEBSITE kidzania.ae
MAP p.214

For something truly unique that will keep the kids entertained for hours (they won't even notice if you sneak off for a spot of shopping), head to KidZania. This fantastic edutainment zone gives children the chance to become adults for the day.

Billed as a 'real-life city' for children, youngsters can dress up and act out more than 80 different roles. After checking in at KidZania International Airport, it's time to head to the bank to open an account, before choosing the first profession to try out. Kids can play everything from the role of policeman or fireman as part of an emergency response team – complete with a fire truck and fake fire – to being a pilot, doctor or a designer taking part in a fashion show. The KidZania city even has its own currency, KidZos, which children can earn on the 'job' and then spend on services within the 'city'. It's intended to be both fun and educational, and gets top marks from little explorers.

The attraction is fully supervised by professional staff, meaning you can leave your children there (as long as they are above 120cm in height) in full confidence. There's a coffee shop and TV room to keep parents entertained, so it's a win-win situation for everyone!

HIGHLIGHTS
Get your 'driver's licence'
Become a fashion designer
Work as a fireman

NEARBY ATTRACTIONS
Stay within The Dubai Mall and take in the views at Burj Khalifa's observation deck, or catch the 1pm Dubai Fountain show.

BEST FOR Families

> **"Kids will love earning and spending the currency, KidZos."**

LITTLE EXPLORERS

WHERE Mirdif City Centre
WHEN Timings vary
HOW MUCH Prices starts at Dhs.100
TIME SPENT Full day
CONTACT 04 80 0386
WEBSITE theplaymania.com
MAP p.215

Little Explorers at Playnation is not your average play centre. Offering an exciting mix of education and entertainment for children from two to seven, this bright and spacious attraction is divided into five zones: I Discover Myself, I Can Do, I Locate Myself, All Together and I Experiment. And each one is jam-packed with fun learning experiences.

There's a fantastic building site with foam bricks, chutes and miniature wheelbarrows, where little construction workers can dress up in hard hats and tabards for role play fun. Kids will love the obstacle course complete with balance beam,

crawling tunnels and wobbly steps, and can experiment in a fun science zone that packs in waterplay alongside air and light exhibits. There's also a zone dedicated to learning about the human body, with fun physical and mental games, as well an area that makes learning letters, numbers, colours and shapes pure child's play.

There are more than 80 different activities in all, including a workshop that runs arts and crafts activities every hour – so more than enough to warrant a full day or a return trip. Passes are available for the day, and you can leave the kids under supervised care while you shop.

HIGHLIGHTS
Building sites
Science experiments
Waterplay area

NEARBY ATTRACTIONS
The indoor 'skydiving' on offer at iFLY Dubai is a heart-thumping activity that's perfect for beginners and seasoned skydivers.

"Little Explorers hosts interactive workshops for young kids."

MAGIC PLANET

WHERE Mall of the Emirates
WHEN Weekdays, 10am-10pm.
Weekends, 10am-12am
HOW MUCH Dhs.85 for a Magic
Planet Passport
TIME SPENT Full day
CONTACT 04 341 4444
WEBSITE magicplanet.ae
MAP p.213

There are numerous branches of this popular entertainment hub located in various malls throughout the UAE, including Mirdif City Centre, Ajman City Centre and Sharjah City Centre, but our favourite is the one at Mall of the Emirates. It's a blaring, boisterous play area that's a firm favourite with kids accompanying their mums and dads on long shopping trips.

To keep the whole family entertained, there are various rides and activities to try out, including merry-go-rounds, a train, bumper cars, bowling lanes and the latest video games. Amusement games give out tickets to collect and exchange for different prizes, which is always popular with kids. For tinier tots there's a large play gym and a small soft play area. Entry is free, and you can use the facilities on a 'pay as you play' basis or buy a Dhs.85 special pass for unlimited fun.

Also housed here is a state-of-the-art XD Theatre – an interactive experience with 3D and 4D effects including motion, wind and light – that immerse you in a variety of exhilarating games, from battling zombies to waging war on pirates. Plus, once you're done having fun at Magic Planet, there's the whole Mall of the Emirates to explore.

HIGHLIGHTS
Bowling lanes
XD Theatre
Bumper cars

NEARBY ATTRACTIONS
Visit the Dubai Community Theatre & Arts Centre (DUCTAC) to see what shows and classes are scheduled.

"Try out the interactive XD Theatre cinema experience."

SHEIKH ZAYED GRAND MOSQUE

WHERE Shk Rashid Bin Saeed Al Maktoum St
WHEN Daily, 9am-10pm. Friday, 4pm-10pm
HOW MUCH Free
TIME SPENT Less than three hours
CONTACT 02 441 6444
WEBSITE szgmc.ae
MAP p.208

BEST FOR **Visitors**

This Abu Dhabi icon is a truly remarkable architectural feat, reminiscent of a sultan's palace from the *Arabian Nights*. Sheikh Zayed Grand Mosque has captivated worshippers and visitors ever since it opened in 2007. An architectural work of art dedicated to the father of the UAE, it never fails to impress.

Once you've marvelled at the gleaming marble exterior, 80 domes and manicured grounds, you can step inside – unlike most mosques in the UAE, it is open to non-Muslims – and take a 45-minute guided tour. Here, you'll find over 1,000 columns, 24-carat gold-plated chandeliers and the world's largest hand-woven Persian carpet. It is one the largest mosques in the world – the main prayer hall can accommodate an astonishing 7,000 worshippers.

Dress codes are strict so make sure you wear long, loose-fitting garments covering your wrists and ankles. Women must wear an abaya; these are provided free of charge at the mosque. Whether you want to learn more about Islam or simply see this masterpiece up close, a visit to Sheikh Zayed Grand Mosque is a must. Note that that the mosque is closed during call to prayer, prayer times and on the first day of Eid Al Fitr and Eid Al Adha.

HIGHLIGHTS
Guided tour
Main prayer hall
Views from the entrance

NEARBY ATTRACTIONS
Visit the mosque as part of the Abu Dhabi Big Bus Tour and go on to Manarat Al Saadiyat and BAKE beach club on Saadiyat Island.

"Admire the world's largest hand-woven Persian carpet."

AL JAHILI FORT

WHERE Nr Central Public Gardens
WHEN Saturday to Thursday,
9am-5pm. Friday, 3pm-5pm.
Closed Mondays
HOW MUCH Free
TIME SPENT Less than three hours
CONTACT 03 784 3996
WEBSITE abudhabi.ae
MAP p.210

The impressive Al Jahili Fort is over 100 years old and one of the UAE's largest forts. Celebrated as the birthplace of the late Sheikh Zayed bin Sultan Al Nahyan, the picturesque fort was erected in the 1890s to defend Al Ain's precious palm groves. Following recent extensive renovation, it is set in beautifully landscaped gardens that are well worth exploring.

It's also the stunning venue for a number of concerts during the Abu Dhabi Classics series (abudhabiclassics. com) as well as one-off events and exhibitions. Be sure to check out the permanent exhibition on British explorer Wilfred Thesiger

(affectionately referred to locally as Mubarak bin London), including memoirs and photos of his 1940s crossings of the Rub Al Khali desert.

If Al Jahili's distinctive three-tiered fort seems familiar, it could well be due to its appearance on the UAE's Dhs.50 note. Not only has it made its mark on the country's currency, the building also won the International Architecture Award in 2010, thanks to its combination of old and new technologies to create a heritage building capable of hosting modern activities. It's an important national landmark, and an atmospheric place to explore.

HIGHLIGHTS
Wilfred Thesiger exhibition
Landscaped gardens
Picturesque courtyards

NEARBY ATTRACTIONS
Get back to nature with a hike (or drive) to the summit of Jebel Hafeet, or enjoy the watersports at Wadi Adventure.

"See the permanent exhibition on explorer Wilfred Thesiger."

JUMEIRAH MOSQUE

WHERE Jumeira Road
WHEN Daily, 10am (except Fridays)
HOW MUCH Dhs.10
TIME SPENT Less than three hours
CONTACT 04 353 6666
WEBSITE cultures.ae
MAP p.214

The much-photographed Jumeirah Mosque is one of Dubai's most famous landmarks and the only mosque in the emirate that allows non-Muslims inside. The best way for visitors to view the mosque is by taking a tour with the Sheikh Mohammed Centre for Cultural Understanding.

The centre organises mosque tours for non-Muslims everyday at 10am except for Fridays. You'll be guided around the impressive building – whose image features on the Dhs.500 note – followed by a talk on Islam and prayer rituals. It's an excellent way to learn more about the mosque itself as well as the culture and beliefs of the local population. Large groups have the option of booking a private tour. Whichever option you go for, the tour lasts around 90 minutes, followed by a Q&A session.

There are a couple of things to take into consideration when planning your visit. Pre-booking is recommended and there is a registration fee of Dhs.10. Also, it is essential that you dress conservatively; both men and women should avoid wearing shorts or sleeveless tops, women must cover their heads with a scarf or shawl, and all visitors must remove their shoes before entering the mosque.

HIGHLIGHTS
Guided tour
View from Hugo's cafe opposite
Photo opportunities at sunset

NEARBY ATTRACTIONS
The Sheikh Mohammed Centre for Cultural Understanding holds regular events including creekside tours and traditional meals.

"Photography *is* allowed inside the mosque, so bring a camera."

FUJAIRAH FORT

WHERE Nr Fujairah Heritage Village
WHEN Timings vary
HOW MUCH Free
TIME SPENT Less than three hours
WEBSITE fujairahtourism.ae
MAP p.211

The majestic Fujairah Fort is one of the oldest and most important in the emirate, as well as being among the most photographed. It's an impressive building located on a raised hilltop overlooking the city and just a few kilometres from the sea. The fort is thought to have been erected in the early 16th century and then rebuilt in the late 17th century. More recently, the fort was renovated by the Department of Antiquities and Heritage, who used the same materials that it was originally built from to maintain its authenticity.

Although you can't enter Fujairah Fort itself, the surrounding heritage buildings are open to the public, and the nearby remains of traditional houses are easily viewed. Architecture fans will find plenty to appreciate from the outside of the fort anyway, as its three circular towers and fourth square tower make it quite an anomaly compared to the more angular forts that the UAE is known for.

To learn even more about the emirate's history, visit Fujairah Heritage Village nearby to see traditional houses and fishing boats. There's also Bidiyah Mosque, one of the oldest mosques in the UAE, which makes for gorgeous photos against the backdrop of the Hajar Mountains.

HIGHLIGHTS
Views from the top of the steps
Unusual architecture

NEARBY ATTRACTIONS
Fujairah has a number of traditional attractions just waiting to be discovered at Fujairah Heritage Village.

"Visit nearby Bidyah Mosque, one of the oldest in the emirate."

HERITAGE VILLAGE

WHERE Nr Marina Mall
WHEN Saturday to Thursday,
9am-5pm. Fridays, 3.30pm-9pm
HOW MUCH Free
TIME SPENT Less than three hours
CONTACT 02 681 4455
WEBSITE torath.ae
MAP p.208

The Heritage Village is a particularly quirky find located near Marina Mall facing Abu Dhabi's waterfront. Run by the Emirates Heritage Club, it's a reconstruction of a traditional oasis village where visitors can get a taste of what Emirati life used to be like. Various aspects of the traditional Bedouin way of life, including a camp fire with coffee pots, a goats' hair tent, a drinking well and a falaj irrigation system, are attractively displayed in the open museum.

Although there is not a great deal of information available in terms of what era or area the relics come from, this is more than made up for by the lively displays on offer. There are workshops where craftsmen demonstrate traditional skills, such as metal work and pottery, while women sit weaving and spinning. They are happy to share their skills and may even give you the chance to try them out or purchase some of their wares.

The spice shop is a great place to buy saffron; the world's most expensive spice is available at far less than you'd pay in major supermarkets, and there are market stalls selling fabric and jewellery too. After visiting the village, sample some typical Arabic cuisine at the waterside restaurant with great views of the Corniche.

HIGHLIGHTS
Spice shop
Souvenir market
Craft workshops

NEARBY ATTRACTIONS
Indulge in some retail therapy at Marina Mall, stroll along the seafront or enjoy a beach day along Abu Dhabi Corniche.

"Be sure to pick up some souvenirs at the outdoor market stalls."

HERITAGE & DIVING VILLAGES

WHERE Nr Sheikh Saeed
Al Maktoum House
WHEN Saturday to Thursday,
8.30am-10pm. Fridays, 3.30pm-10pm
HOW MUCH Free
TIME SPENT Less than three hours
CONTACT 04 393 7139
WEBSITE definitelydubai.com
MAP p.215

BEST FOR
History

For a fascinating glimpse into Dubai's rich history, particularly its maritime past, the Heritage and Diving Villages are an excellent spot to spend the afternoon. Located near the mouth of Dubai Creek, this cultural attraction focuses on Dubai's maritime past, pearl diving trade, arts, customs and architecture. Here you can observe traditional potters and weavers practising their crafts the way they have been done for centuries.

It's also a rare opportunity to get close to local wildlife such as falcons and camels, or sample genuine Emirati cuisine as local women in traditional dress serve up authentic snacks.

For the most part, the villages are relatively quiet; the best and liveliest time to visit is during the Dubai Shopping Festival or Eid celebrations, when they come alive with a variety of exciting performances including traditional sword dancing.

Once you've had your fill of the villages, head to nearby Sheikh Saeed Al Maktoum House, the home of the much-loved former ruler of Dubai. As one of the oldest residences in the city, it's a good example of a traditional home with sheltered courtyards and spacious majlis. It also houses a number of interesting photographic exhibits and relics from the past.

HIGHLIGHTS
Craft demonstrations
Traditional coffee house
Festival performances

NEARBY ATTRACTIONS
The Dubai Creek area is a far cry from the skyscrapers of the city centre and an interesting neighbourhood to explore.

"Check out the old photographs of pearl divers in the village."

FUJAIRAH HERITAGE VILLAGE

WHERE Nr Fujairah Fort
WHEN Timings vary
HOW MUCH Free
TIME SPENT Half day
WEBSITE fujmun.gov.ae
MAP p.211

Situated just outside of Fujairah city, this purpose-built village takes you back in time to experience traditional life in the emirate. Walk around the village and see firsthand the realities of what Bedouin life was like in the unforgiving desert climate. The village is home to a collection of fishing boats, simple dhows and tools that depicts everyday life in the UAE before oil was discovered.

Be sure to keep an eye out for the ox-driven waterwheels that were used to irrigate date palm plantations, and the sea fishing nets made from palm fibres, as well as other rudimentary forms of technology that were once a part of everyday life. You'll learn about traditional Emirati dance, and get a detailed insight into the ritual of how Arabic coffee is made, right down to the roasting of the coffee beans. After a morning of cultural immersion, you can stay and relax in the sun, as there are two spring-fed swimming pools for men and women, and chalets that can be hired for the day.

While you're in the area, be sure to pay a visit to nearby Fujairah Fort. One of the oldest forts in the UAE, it's thought to date back to the 16th century and is a fine example of traditional architecture with its towers, courtyards and majlis.

HIGHLIGHTS
Traditional dhows
Ox-driven waterwheels
Sea fishing nets

NEARBY ATTRACTIONS
The area boasts a number of historic attractions including Fujairah Fort, Fujairah Museum and Fujairah National Park.

"Soak up some sun then cool down in a spring-fed swimming pool."

SHARJAH HERITAGE AREA

WHERE Nr Al Mareija & Corniche St
WHEN Timings vary
HOW MUCH Prices vary
TIME SPENT Full day
WEBSITE sharjahtourism.ae
MAP p.218

Soak up some old-world Arabia with a wander round Sharjah Heritage Area. Also known as the Heart of Sharjah, it is the region's largest heritage project, dedicated to restoration and renovation. Some of the buildings date back more than 200 years and have been lovingly preserved.

Be sure to check out Majlis Al Midfaa, an iconic round windtower at the heart of the Heritage Area. Established 80 years ago, it is the birthplace of the country's first newspaper, which you can learn more at the museum there. Several other museums in the area are worth a look, including Al Eslah

School Museum where classrooms are kept as they were in 1935 when it was Sharjah's first school. Sharjah Calligraphy Museum explores this important traditional art form, while the 160-year-old Bait Al Naboodah is a beautiful old house at which to learn about Emirati life in the 19th century. Sharjah Heritage Museum is well worth a visit to see some excellent exhibitions too.

Mostly though, the experience is about wandering around the cobbled squares and coral-walled alleyways, past ornately carved doors, pretty lanterns and fascinating architecture, and imagining a bygone world.

HIGHLIGHTS
Sharjah Heritage Museum
Bait Al Naboodah
Majlis Al Midfaa

NEARBY ATTRACTIONS
Visit Souk Al Arsah where the shops are packed with curiosities, including daggers and old coins, as well as the usual tourist souvenirs.

"Visit Al Eslah School Museum to see traditional classrooms."

DOWNTOWN DUBAI

WHERE Downtown Dubai
WHEN Timings vary
HOW MUCH Prices vary
TIME SPENT Full day
WEBSITE mydowntowndubai.com
MAP p.214

In many ways, Downtown Dubai epitomises everything that the emirate is best known for: mind-boggling architecture, luxurious attractions and some of the finest dining spots in the city. Needless to say, it's the perfect place to spend a day with visitors, or anyone new to the UAE.

The biggest attraction is undoubtedly the record-breaking Burj Khalifa. To truly appreciate this iconic 163-storey tower, head for At The Top, the building's observation deck. In less than 60 seconds, a high-speed lift travelling at 10 metres per second will transport you to the 124th floor, where the floor-to-ceiling windows afford an incredible 360° view of the city. It's well worth planning your trip ahead of time, especially if you're visiting on the weekend when it can get very busy. Advance bookings are Dhs.100 for adults and Dhs.75 for children, whereas tickets bought on the day cost from Dhs.400.

Time your visit with the impressive Dubai Fountain water, music and light shows, which take place at 1pm and 1.30pm daily. Round off your day with a visit to the Arabian-inspired Souk Al Bahar – home to waterfront cafes and restaurants, as well as souvenir and boutique shops where you can pick up a memento of your trip.

HIGHLIGHTS
At The Top at Burj Khalifa
The Dubai Fountain show
Souk Al Bahar

NEARBY ATTRACTIONS
The Dubai Mall is packed with attractions, including KidZania, a cinema, ice rink and indoor theme park SEGA Republic.

"Time your visit to coincide with the Dubai Fountain show."

EMIRATES NATIONAL AUTO MUSEUM

WHERE Hamim Rd
WHEN Timings vary
HOW MUCH Dhs.50.
Children under 10 get free entry
TIME SPENT Less than three hours
CONTACT 050 810 2211
WEBSITE enam.ae
MAP p.209

If you're looking for a low-key afternoon out of the city, the Emirates National Auto Museum certainly fits the bill. While lacking in the gargantuan glamour of Yas Island's Ferrari World, the museum still makes for a great day out, whether you're a motoring enthusiast or not.

Within the impressive pyramid-shaped building, you'll find an incredible private collection belonging to Sheikh Hamad bin Hamdan Al Nahyan, also sometimes known as the 'Rainbow Sheikh'. It's an astounding selection of automobiles, with one of the highlights being the Sheikh's rainbow collection of Mercedes.

The vast five-metre high dodge, which houses a complete apartment under its roof, is also an impressive sight. Originally opened in 2005, the automobile museum is home to almost 200 vehicles, including racing car prototypes, classic American cars and off-road vehicles, not to mention the largest truck in the world.

It's such an impressive exhibition, in fact, that some of the collection was showcased in the BBC TV programme *Top Gear*. What's more, the museum's location just 45km outside of Abu Dhabi makes it the perfect pit stop if you're travelling towards picturesque Liwa for a day trip.

HIGHLIGHTS
Rainbow Mercedes collection
Giant Dodge
Racing car prototypes

NEARBY ATTRACTIONS
If a visit to the museum leaves you longing to hit the track, try a driving experience at Yas Marina Circuit on Yas Island.

"Marvel at the Rainbow Sheikh's multi-coloured Mercedes collection."

AJMAN MUSEUM

WHERE Al Bustan
WHEN Daily, 8am-8pm except Fridays and public holidays
HOW MUCH Dhs.5 (adults) Dhs.15 (family)
TIME SPENT Less than three hours
MAP p.207

No trip to Ajman would be complete without a visit to the Ajman Museum. This attractive building is based in a fort thought to have originally been built during the late 18th century, although various battles saw it rebuilt numerous times before it finally became a museum in the 1980s.

This popular cultural attraction houses an astounding collection of artefacts and archaeological finds, including centuries-old manuscripts, weaponry and pottery. There is a good mix of indoor and outdoor exhibitions; in the spacious courtyard you can see recreations of traditional wells, irrigation systems called falaj and the wooden dhows that Ajman was once famous for. Inside, there are intricately detailed models depicting Ajman's culture and history, from family homes and fishing fleets to courts and policing, providing the perfect insight into traditional Emirati life.

One of the many museum highlights is its exhibition on the pearl trade, a period of history that was essential to Ajman's development; the display is a combination of life-sized models and genuine gems and artefacts. It's one of many large scale models depicting traditional life. Other highlights include remains from a cemetery dating back to 3,000 BC.

BEST FOR
History

HIGHLIGHTS
Pearl trade display
Traditional dhows
Falaj irrigation system

NEARBY ATTRACTIONS
Ajman has some great shopping spots: buy some bling at the Gold Souk or pick up the catch of the day at the Fish Market.

"See relics from a cemetery dating back to 3,000 BC."

AL AIN NATIONAL MUSEUM

WHERE Zayed Bin Sultan St
WHEN Saturday to Thursday, 8am-7.30pm. Friday, 3pm-7.30pm
HOW MUCH Dhs.3 (adults) Dhs.1 (children under 10)
TIME SPENT Less than three hours
CONTACT 03 764 1595
WEBSITE abudhabi.ae
MAP p.210

Al Ain National Museum is the oldest museum in the UAE, having opened in 1971 during the country's inaugural year, and is divided into three main sections just waiting to be explored.

The ethnography section focuses on traditional life in the UAE and looks at culture and pastimes, and includes some fascinating old photographs. This section also holds exhibits on falconry and weaponry, as well as two of the UAE's most historically important trades: pearl diving and fishing. Curiosities on display include jewellery and old coins.

In the archaeology section there are examples of Stone Age, Bronze Age and Iron Age objects that were excavated from local sites around Al Ain, including Hili Archaeological Park. Pottery, vessels, copper and bronze jewellery all give an insight into local life thousands of years ago. There's also a reconstruction of a falaj irrigation system, which you can still see in the palm plantations around Al Ain today.

Finally, make sure you check out the 'gifts' section, which hosts some weird and wonderful items that were presented to Sheikh Zayed by visiting dignitaries – there are golden palm trees and ornamental camels. A very interesting display.

HIGHLIGHTS
Historical photographs
Old jewellery and coins
Gifts section

NEARBY ATTRACTIONS
Combine your visit with a trip to the Al Ain Palace Museum and round off the day with a picnic in Al Jahili Park.

"Learn about the region's traditional weaponry and falconry."

AL AIN PALACE MUSEUM

WHERE Central District
WHEN Weekdays, 8:30am-7.30 pm.
Friday, 3pm-7.30pm
HOW MUCH Free
TIME SPENT Less than three hours
CONTACT 03 751 7755
WEBSITE abudhabi.ae
MAP p.210

This fascinating museum, which dates back to 1937, was originally a palace belonging to Sheikh Zayed bin Sultan Al Nahyan. Today it tells the story of the founding ruler of the UAE and his remarkable achievements, as well as offering an insight into his upbringing and palace life.

Guided tours here are free and highly recommended, and the Emirati guides are proud and knowledgeable. You'll learn about Emirati traditions and the culture in general, and gain a real sense of time and place. Everyday items from a bygone era are displayed around the various rooms you can wander through; these include rooms

for palace guests and dignitaries, women's quarters, storerooms, coffee houses, guards' rooms, majlis, the palace school rooms and some spiritual rooms.

Be sure to check out the Al Nahyan family tree, which dates as far back as Eissa Bin Nahyan in the 18th century. Also, take a peek down the traditional water well, which is encircled by a stone wall and straddled by palm tree struts and a winch that carries a goat's bladder bucket to collect the water below. Overall, the museum is a lovely, quiet place to stroll and explore, and a great place to bring children and spend an afternoon.

HIGHLIGHTS
Informative family tree
Guided tour
Traditional well

NEARBY ATTRACTIONS
History buffs will also enjoy Al Ain National Museum and Al Jahili Fort. Round off the afternoon with a BBQ in Al Jahili Park.

"Be sure to take a guided tour to learn more about the region."

HILI ARCHAEOLOGICAL PARK

WHERE Mohd Ibn Khalifa St
WHEN Saturday to Thursday,
4:30pm-9:30pm. Friday, 10am-10pm
HOW MUCH Dhs.1
TIME SPENT Less than three hours
WEBSITE abudhabi.ae
MAP p.210

The city of Al Ain may not be as well known a destination as neighbouring Abu Dhabi or Dubai, but it boasts one of the most significant heritage sites in the UAE. Located 12km outside Al Ain on the Dubai-Al Ain highway, Hili Archaeological Park is home to the remnants of a mud-brick Bronze Age settlement from the Umm An Nar period, which dates back to around 2,700-2,000 BC.

The park was excavated and restored in 1995. One of the tombs found here, known as the Grand Garden Tomb, held the remains of almost 250 people, along with a host of burial treasures including jewellery, tools and ceramics. Many of the artefacts found during the excavation can today be seen on display at the Al Ain National Museum.

The park site is part of the larger Al Hili village area, which is rumoured to be the largest Bronze Age site in the UAE and a globally important historical site. The oldest falaj system in the UAE was found here, and you'll find all manner of insights into the culture and livelihood of the people that lived here thousands of years ago. And, history aside, the charming gardens here are simply a pleasant walk in their own right, especially during the cooler months.

HIGHLIGHTS
Grand Garden Tomb
Al Hili village area
Archaeological relics

NEARBY ATTRACTIONS
Hili Fun City is a great place to spend the rest of your day, with theme park rides, BBQ spots and shaded picnic areas.

"Visit the Grand Garden Tomb, which held a host of buried treasures."

DUBAI MOVING IMAGE MUSEUM

WHERE MCN Hive Bldg, TECOM
WHEN Timings vary
HOW MUCH Dhs.50 (adults)
Dhs.25 (children)
TIME SPENT Less than three hours
CONTACT 04 421 6679
WEBSITE dubaimovingimage
museum.com
MAP p.213

Hidden away in TECOM is this wonderful addition to Dubai's cultural scene. The museum charts the history of the moving image prior to the advent of cinema, with the invention of the camera attributed to Arab scientist Ibn al-Haythem's 11th century creation of 'Al Qumra'.

An incredible array of lovingly preserved antiques, some from as early as 1730, are presented in displays lining this clean, modern space. The museum explores how light and shadow have been played with to create moving images for millennia – from the shadow puppets of ancient civilisations, to the creation of multiple frame photography that makes us see movement in a succession of still images. These precursors to the snapshots that bombard our Facebook pages today were entertaining astonished punters in the 18th century.

And there's a lot to try out too – while most of the antiques are kept safely behind glass, there are some cool reproductions to play with, optical illusions, and videos to watch. You can spin the handle on an original Mutoscope and watch Charlie Chaplin, or there are 19th century contraptions that created crisp 3D images long before *Avatar* hit our screens – take a peek into the Kaiser Panorama.

HIGHLIGHTS
Kaiser Panorama
19th century magic lanterns
Shadow puppets

NEARBY ATTRACTIONS
Visit the nearby Ibn Battuta Mall which is packed with attractions including shops, play centres, cafes and an IMAX movie theatre.

"Pay an additional Dhs.10 and enjoy a fascinating guided tour."

DUBAI MUSEUM

WHERE Al Souk Al Kabeer
WHEN Daily, 8.30am-8.30pm.
Friday, 2.30pm-8.30pm
HOW MUCH Dhs.3 (adults) Dhs.1
(children under six)
TIME SPENT Less than three hours
CONTACT 04 353 1862
WEBSITE definitelydubai.com
MAP p.215

Dubai's older neighbourhoods reveal a completely different side to the emirate – far away from the busy shopping malls and sparkling skyscrapers, you'll find a myriad of cultural attractions, including the Dubai Museum. Housed in Al Fahidi Fort, a traditional Arabic fort that dates back to 1780, this family-friendly museum was once the home of the ruler of Dubai and also functioned as a sea defence.

This impressive building has stood as a museum since its renovation in the early 1970s and today it houses all manner of interesting artefacts and relics from Dubai's past. Galleries and dioramas have been used to depict life from a bygone era; you'll find souks from the 1950s, stroll through an oasis, step into a traditional house and even get up close to local wildlife. There's also an 'underwater' section depicting the pearl diving and fishing industries. It's a great budget option with tickets costing just Dhs.3 for adults and Dhs.1 for children under six, and there's enough to keep kids entertained, including some fun mannequins to pose with.

Dubai Museum is also one of the stops on the Dubai Big Bus Tour route, and free entry is included in the price of a bus tour ticket.

HIGHLIGHTS
Souks
Pearl and fishing display
Multimedia show

NEARBY ATTRACTIONS
Visit the Dubai Museum as part of the Big Bus Tour, which includes stops at Dubai Creek and Al Fahidi Historical Neighbourhood.

"Visit the 'underwater' section to learn about the pearling trade."

SHEIKH SAEED AL MAKTOUM HOUSE

WHERE Nr Heritage & Diving Villages
WHEN Saturday to Thursday, 8.30am-8.30pm. Friday, 3pm-8.30pm
HOW MUCH Dhs.2 (adults) Dhs.1 (children)
TIME SPENT Less than three hours
CONTACT 04 393 7139
WEBSITE definitelydubai.com
MAP p.215

BEST FOR
History

For a fascinating insight into traditional Islamic architecture and Emirati history, head for Sheikh Saeed Al Maktoum House. This 19th century restored house-turned-museum was constructed in a way typical of the time and era, using coral covered in lime and sand-coloured plaster.

Located in Shindagha, one of the oldest neighbourhoods in Dubai, the house was once home to the visionary leader Sheikh Saeed Al Maktoum. Centuries ago it provided the ruling family with unparalled views of the shipbuilding district and Arabian Gulf.

Also known as the Al Shindagha Museum, today Sheikh Saeed Al

Maktoum House is home to an impressive collection of Emirati artefacts including historical documents and maps, and wonderful rare photographs that capture the Dubai of a bygone era.

When you're not wandering through the courtyard or admiring the traditional windtowers, there are plenty of displays to peruse recounting traditional Emirati life. Be sure to factor enough time into your visit to check out the nearby Dubai Heritage and Diving Villages, where artists and craftsmen display their wares, and the emirate's rich maritime history is showcased.

HIGHLIGHTS
Rare photographs
Coin collection
Traditional architecture

NEARBY ATTRACTIONS
Head for Dubai's Heritage and Diving Villages to see traditional arts and crafts, as well as displays on fishing and pearl diving.

"Admire the view over Dubai Creek from the upper floor."

FUJAIRAH MUSEUM

WHERE Nr Fujairah Heritage Village, Al Sharia
WHEN Saturday to Thursday, 8am-6.30pm. Friday, 2pm-6.30pm
HOW MUCH Dhs.5
TIME SPENT Less than three hours
CONTACT 09 222 9085
MAP p.211

This interesting museum has a number of permanent exhibitions that explore traditional ways of life in Fujairah and the UAE, including the not-so-distant nomadic Bedouin culture. As you peruse the displays, you'll learn about the heritage, customs and traditional livelihoods of Fujairah. There's a heavy emphasis on farming – unusually for the UAE, agriculture has played a large part in the economic history of the emirate, which is by far the most fertile area of the UAE.

There are several artefacts on display that were found during archaeological excavations at various sites throughout Fujairah, some of which date back as far as 5,000BC. These include discoveries at the villages of Al Bithna and Qidfa. The collection is sure to impress history buffs, with items on display including weapons from the bronze and iron ages, finely painted pottery, carved soapstone vessels, spearheads and silver coins.

Fujairah is home to a number of other heritage sites, so make sure you factor in enough time to visit Fujairah Fort, located just north of the museum. For a full day of cultural immersion, combine both with a visit to Fujairah Heritage Village and Fujairah National Park.

HIGHLIGHTS
Heritage displays
Ancient pottery
Bronze Age weapons

NEARBY ATTRACTIONS
After you've had your fill of the museum, head for Fujairah Fort, set against the stunning backdrop of the Hajar Mountains.

"Don't miss the exhibition on ancient folkloric medicine."

NATIONAL MUSEUM OF RAS AL KHAIMAH

WHERE Nr Police HQ
WHEN Weekdays, 9am-6pm.
Friday, 3pm-7.30pm
HOW MUCH Dhs.5 (adults)
Dhs.2 (children), Dhs.10 (families)
TIME SPENT Less than three hours
CONTACT 07 233 3411
WEBSITE rasalkhaimahtourism.com
MAP p.216

BEST FOR History

Housed in an impressive fort that was once the home of the present ruler of Ras Al Khaimah, Sheikh Saud Bin Saqr Al Qasimi, this museum focuses on local natural history and archaeological displays that include a variety of paraphernalia from pre-oil, Bedouin life. History lovers should keep an eye out for fossils set into the rock strata of the walls of the fort – these are thought to date back 190 million years. The building has battlements, a working windtower and ornate, carved wooden doors.

The National Museum of Ras Al Khaimah is just one of several interesting historical sites located throughout the northernmost emirate – look out for Shimal Archaeological Site, which includes a tomb from the Umm An Nar period, roughly 5,000 years ago. Built as a communal burial place, the remains of more than 400 bodies have been found there.

Also worth visiting are Dhayah Fort and Sheba's Palace. Many of the findings from these sites are housed in the National Museum. Another museum in Ras Al Khaimah well worth checking out is the Pearl Museum on Al Qawasim Corniche, where you can learn about the emirate's illustrious pearling history and its relationship with the Arabian Gulf.

HIGHLIGHTS
A working windtower
Local architecture
Ancient fossils

NEARBY ATTRACTIONS
To learn more about the emirate's history, head for Dhayah Fort. Or, for a more frivolous afternoon, unwind at Ice Land Water Park.

"Look for Shimal Archaeological Site's 5,000-year-old tomb."

SHARJAH ARCHAEOLOGY MUSEUM

WHERE Near Cultural Square, Al Abar
WHEN Saturday, Monday to Thursday,
8am-8pm. Friday, 4pm-8pm
HOW MUCH Dhs.5 (adults), Dhs.10
(families). Free entry for children
TIME SPENT Less than three hours
CONTACT 06 566 5466
WEBSITE sharjahmuseums.ae
MAP p.218

This impressive, hi-tech museum is accessible and informative for all, and well worth a visit for culture buffs. Using well-designed displays and documentary film, the museum traces man's progress across the Arabian Peninsula through the ages.

There's an interesting display of antiquities, including pottery, weapons and jewellery from throughout the region. Of particular note are the exhibits from excavation sites in Sharjah itself, which the museum deals with brilliantly. The artefacts reveal that nomadic tribes were hunting, fishing and herding in Sharjah an astonishing 7,000 years ago.

The oldest evidence of early human subsistence in the UAE comes from Jebel Faya in Sharjah, which dates back to 85,000 BC and supports the 'out of Africa' migration theory. Stone Age and Iron Age multi-chambered graves at Jebel al-Buhais reveal a surprising amount about ancient ways of life, while the fascinating camel and horse cemetery at Mleih illustrates the historical importance of these animals, which were adorned with gold and buried with their owners.

You might even be inspired to spend the afternoon visiting the sites themselves, making for a day trip that you're sure to 'dig'.

HIGHLIGHTS
Stone Age relics
Gold-decorated horse harness
Flint arrowhead collection

NEARBY ATTRACTIONS
For more insight into the emirate's past, visit the Sharjah Museum of Islamic Civilization or wander around the Sharjah Heritage Area.

"Take part in an informative guided tour of the museum."

SHARJAH CLASSIC CAR MUSEUM

WHERE Al Dhaid-Sharjah Road
WHEN Saturday, Monday to Thursday, 8am-8pm. Friday, 4pm-8pm
HOW MUCH Dhs.5 (adults) Dhs.15 (families)
TIME SPENT Less than three hours
CONTACT 06 558 0222
WEBSITE sharjahmuseums.ae
MAP p.219

This fantastic and well-curated museum is definitely worth a visit, whether or not you are 'into' cars. There's a large number of vehicles on display, all beautifully presented and all dating from 1979 or earlier. Many of the cars are from His Highness Sheikh Dr Sultan Bin Mohammad Al Qasimi's personal collection, including a 1934 Rolls Royce.

There's a beautifully maintained 1915 Dodge, notable for its wooden wheels, and from here it's a journey through the history of the automobile. A fabulous green and gold E-model Ford from 1918 sits alongside Fiat's funky orange 509 from the 1920s.

Moving through the 40s and 50s, there are Plymouths, a Suburban, and, impressively, the same Cadillac Coupe model that was driven by Elvis Presley. Utility vehicles, an ambulance and even a collection of Penny Farthing bicycles add to the breadth of the collection.

As well as appreciating each car and its historical value, the exhibits provide information on the socio-economic factors that influenced the evolution of the car, and its place in society as more than just a transportation device. Displays are quirky, fun and well-presented – it's a great place to soak up some history and to impress any auto enthusiasts.

HIGHLIGHTS
1915 Dodge
E-model Ford
Cadillac Coupe

NEARBY ATTRACTIONS
The Sharjah Discovery Centre is the perfect place to round off a family day out, thanks to its interactive, kid-friendly displays.

"See an old-fashioned ambulance, and 1960s British Triumph."

SHARJAH DISCOVERY CENTRE

WHERE Al Dhaid-Sharjah Road
WHEN Sunday to Thursday, 8am-2pm.
Friday and Saturday, 4pm-8pm
HOW MUCH Dhs.10 (adults) Dhs.5
(children). Free (children under three)
TIME SPENT Full day
CONTACT 06 558 6577
WEBSITE sharjahmuseums.ae
MAP p.219

BEST FOR
Families

This science-based play centre is an immensely fun place to take the kids. A big, bright, colourful hall filled with different activities, the Discovery Centre is divided into educational zones – but it's really more about playing and having fun, with a bit of learning thrown in.

In the Body Zone, there's a climbing frame that replicates blood-flow through the heart, as well as the opportunity to test reaction, strength and peripheral vision. Over in Build Town, kids can operate cranes, conveyors and chutes to move materials around a construction site. At Sharjah International Kids Airport,

you can simulate the travel experience with luggage check-in and bag scanners, before donning some wings and taking off on a journey through the clouds that concludes with a slide to replicate 'landing'.

The star attraction is undoubtedly Drive Town and its electric cars, where children learn the rules of the road and then navigate the roundabouts and traffic lights of the driving track. There's also Sports World, which has soccer, basketball and a climbing wall. The centre has a cafe serving snacks and refreshments, and a lovely, large lawn area with picnic benches surrounding the area.

HIGHLIGHTS
Drive Town
Sharjah International Kids Airport
Body Zone

NEARBY ATTRACTIONS
Enjoy more edutainment at the Sharjah Science Museum or get back to nature at Arabia's Wildlife Centre.

"Kids can get behind the wheel of electric cars in Drive Town."

SHARJAH HERITAGE MUSEUM

WHERE Sharjah Heritage Area
WHEN Saturday to Thursday, 8am-8pm. Friday, 4pm-8pm
HOW MUCH Dhs.5 (adults) Dhs.10 (families)
TIME SPENT Less than three hours
CONTACT 06 568 0006
WEBSITE sharjahmuseums.ae
MAP p.218

Step back into the UAE's past with a visit to Sharjah Heritage Museum. This popular attraction is housed in an old pearl merchant's home dating back to around 1795 – Bait Saeed Al Taweel Al Shamsi, the house of Saeed bin Mohammed Al Shamsi.

While some of the original features have been lost or damaged over the years, including one of its three towers, the building was renovated in the 1990s and today sits in the heart of the atmospheric Heritage Area. The museum's six galleries focus on landscape, lifestyle, celebrations, livelihood, traditional knowledge and oral traditions. The displays are lively,

with plenty of interesting information on traditional Emirati customs, the effect of Islam on the local way of life, and timeless Bedouin traditions such as desert survival and navigation.

An interactive gallery displays the UAE's heritage in proverbs, popular riddles and children's stories. Videos showing children singing traditional songs give an affecting feel to the museum, especially as you are unlikely to share it with many other people, if any. It is deserving of your attention though, especially when combined with a stroll around the Heritage Area and a peek into the other museums here.

HIGHLIGHTS
Cinema
Oral traditions gallery
Interactive heritage displays

NEARBY ATTRACTIONS
The rest of the Sharjah Heritage Area is worth exploring, as is the Sharjah Art Museum, which is just a short stroll away.

"Enjoy the views of Sharjah Heritage Area from the rooftop."

SHARJAH MARITIME MUSEUM

WHERE Nr Sharjah Aquarium, Al Khan
WHEN Saturday to Thursday, 8am-8pm. Friday, 4pm-8pm
HOW MUCH Dhs.8 (adults), Dhs.4 (children), Dhs.20 (families)
TIME SPENT Less than three hours
CONTACT 06 522 2002
WEBSITE sharjahmuseums.ae
MAP p.218

This bright and airy tribute to Sharjah's seafaring traditions has some superb displays, and is crammed with information on the emirate's illustrious fishing, trading and pearling past. Videos and photography capture the Sharjah of times past, while life-size dhows and displays of maritime equipment are sure to grab your attention.

Genuine Arabian pearls are on display and you can learn about how they were collected, measured and weighed. It's a fascinating insight into the historic trade relations between the Gulf people and the rest of the world, and explores the various subjects that come with spending months at a time at sea, such as navigation by the stars.

The museum is on the site of Al Khan Village, where signs of a Neolithic fishing village were once dug up by archaeologists – there are even plans to create a maritime-themed heritage village here.

The Maritime Museum is adjacent to Sharjah Aquarium, another marine-themed attraction in the emirate that's worth a visit. Tickets to the aquarium include entrance to the Maritime Museum; however, this doesn't work the other way round as the aquarium is a little pricier.

HIGHLIGHTS
Life-size dhow
Video footage and photos
Neolithic fishing village

NEARBY ATTRACTIONS
Enjoy the cafe culture around the canal at Al Qasba or have lunch with a view at a restaurant along Al Majaz Waterfront.

"Be sure to see the genuine pearl diving artefacts on display."

SHARJAH MUSEUM OF ISLAMIC CIVILIZATION

WHERE Corniche St
WHEN Saturday to Thursday, 8am-8pm. Friday, 4pm-8pm
HOW MUCH Dhs.5 (adults) Dhs.10 (families). Free for children
TIME SPENT Less than three hours
CONTACT 06 565 5455
WEBSITE sharjahmuseums.ae
MAP p.218

This vast museum, in UAE terms, housed in the building of a former souk, explores the history of Islam and its incredible influence on the modern world, including science, art, culture and society. It's one of the best places in the country to learn about Islam and Islamic culture. The museum holds more than 5,000 artefacts from across the Muslim world, which are informatively displayed in several different galleries.

The impressive Abu Bakr Gallery of Islamic Faith on the ground floor looks at the Five Pillars of Islam. It's an informative exhibition, and holds some reverent pieces well worth a look

for anyone interested in the Islamic faith; pride of place is a beautiful gold-embroidered curtain for the door of the Holy Ka'ba. Across the hall, the Ibn Al Haitham Gallery for Science and Technology is packed with exhibits illustrating how the importance of scientific exploration in Islamic culture shaped our understanding of the world and formed the basis of a lot of scientific theory.

As well as the permanent collections, the museum hosts well-curated temporary exhibitions, and the ceiling of the central dome is a stunning depiction of the signs of the zodiac – well worth the trip upstairs.

HIGHLIGHTS
Central dome celestial map
Faith Gallery Ka'ba curtain

NEARBY ATTRACTIONS
Visit the Sharjah Art Museum, which is just a short stroll away, then head for Al Majaz Waterfront for an alfresco lunch.

"Don't miss the stunning ceiling dome depiction of the zodiac signs."

SHARJAH NATURAL HISTORY & BOTANICAL MUSEUM

WHERE Sharjah Desert Park
WHEN Timings vary
HOW MUCH Dhs.15 (adults)
Dhs.5 (children)
TIME SPENT Less than three hours
CONTACT 06 531 1411
WEBSITE epaashj.com
MAP p.219

Located 25 kilometres from the city in the Sharjah Desert Park complex, Sharjah Natural History & Botanical Museum is another of the emirate's superb museums, with lively, informative and well-curated exhibits and plenty to keep young visitors engaged. The displays here cover millions of years worth of natural history, and include a piece of the oldest rock in the UAE. This volcanic ash from Sir Bani Yas Island, which is just off the coast of Abu Dhabi, is thought to be 600 million years old.

The journey continues through to the dinosaur era and beyond. There are interactive displays on the relationships between man and the natural world in the UAE, and a fabulous marine-themed room that's designed to make you feel like you're walking underwater.

While you're visiting the Desert Park complex, be sure to check out the quality exhibits at Arabia's Wildlife Centre and meet some furry friends at the Children's Farm, including camels, donkeys and goats. Children will love the chance to feed and pet the animals there. Entrance to the Desert Park covers all three attractions, each of which has its own cafe; the one at Arabia's Wildlife Centre is highly recommended.

HIGHLIGHTS
Interactive displays
Dinosaur exhibition
Marine-themed room

NEARBY ATTRACTIONS
The Sharjah Discovery Centre is a wonderfully kid-friendly attraction, as is the petting farm at Arabia's Wildlife Centre.

"Check out the rock thought to be 600 million years old."

SHARJAH SCIENCE MUSEUM

WHERE Nr Cultural Square, Al Abar
WHEN Sunday to Thursday, 8pm-2pm.
Friday and Saturday, 4pm-8pm
HOW MUCH Dhs.10 (adults), Dhs.5
(children aged three to 17)
TIME SPENT Less than three hours
CONTACT 06 566 8777
WEBSITE sharjahmuseums.ae
MAP p.218

The Sharjah Science Museum was the first interactive science centre to open in the UAE, and remains one of its best. Exhibits and demonstrations at the museum cover a range of interesting subjects including aerodynamics, cryogenics, electricity and colour, while managing to make them fun, friendly and fascinating for all ages.

Tried and tested experiments are sure to impress younger visitors, such as the hilariously hair-raising Van de Graaf machine. There are a number of other astonishing, not to mention interactive demonstrations, that involve some little helpers and audience participation.

One of the major draws of the museum is its superb planetarium, where you'll be taken on an adventure through the solar system, and learn about the connection between Arabian history and astronomy.

For very little ones, there's a children's area where the under-fives and their parents can learn together. There's also a soft play area, and a Learning Centre that offers more in-depth programmes on many of the subjects covered in the museum. You can round off your afternoon with a trip to the gift shop, which is packed with cool souvenirs to take home as a memento of your day.

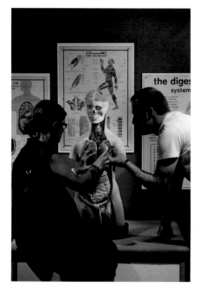

HIGHLIGHTS
Van de Graaf machine
Planetarium
Children's play area

NEARBY ATTRACTIONS
Visit the creative spaces at the Sharjah Art Museum or learn about the emirate's history in the Sharjah Heritage Area.

"Take part in an educational guided tour of the museum."

CHAIRLIFT

DO SOMETHING DIFFERENT

TUBING RUN

SKI SCHOOL

SKIING

SNOW PENGUINS

THE GIANT SNOW BALL

SNOWBOARDING

Looking for an action-packed day out?
Hit the slopes with your skis and snowboards or take on the exciting rides
like The Giant Ball or tubing runs. Or if you're just looking for a place to chill,
come hang out with our adorable Snow Penguins or have a blast at the Snow Park.
There is something for everyone at the coolest destination in town.

Ski Dubai. Do something different.

SKI DUBAI
سكي دبي

Sports & Leisure

KHALIFA INTERNATIONAL BOWLING CENTRE

WHERE Zayed Sports City, Al Madina Al Riyadiya
WHEN Daily, 9am-1am
HOW MUCH Dhs.10 per game
TIME SPENT Less than three hours
CONTACT 02 403 4648
WEBSITE zsc.ae
MAP p.208

Arguably Abu Dhabi's ultimate bowling destination, the Khalifa International Bowling Centre boasts 40 world-class lanes and is reputed to be one of the most modern bowling alleys in the world. Located at Zayed Sports City, the centre was purpose built to international standards in anticipation of the 1999 FIQ 14th World Bowling Championships; it continues to be used by the UAE National Bowling Team even today.

However, you don't have to be a professional to enjoy its world-class bowling facilities. It's a good budget-friendly (as well as family-friendly) activity too, with prices starting from

Dhs.10 per game and shoe hire at an additional Dhs.2. There's always an expert on hand though to offer some bowling tips, as the centre has two certified instructors who are happy to help those who are new to the lanes.

If bowling isn't your thing, the centre is home to Abu Dhabi's largest billiards hall (with 13 tables and prices starting at Dhs.25 per hour), as well as six table tennis tables and a video games arcade, and two pro-shops if you fancy picking up some sporting accessories. There's also a wide selection of food and drink on offer; try the south-east Asian fare at Noodle Bowl.

HIGHLIGHTS
World-class bowling facilities
Billiards hall
Table tennis

NEARBY ATTRACTIONS
Zayed Sports City has a number of places to get active, including the Zayed International Tennis Centre and an ice rink.

"Plan a birthday party at Khalifa International Bowling Centre."

BOWLING CITY

WHERE Dubai Festival City Mall
WHEN Saturday to Wednesday, 10am-midnight. Thursday and Friday, 10am-1am
HOW MUCH Prices start at Dhs.15
TIME SPENT Less than three hours
CONTACT 04 232 8600
WEBSITE bowling-city.com
MAP p.215

For an activity that's guaranteed to entertain the entire family without breaking the bank, it's hard to beat bowling. Over at Dubai Festival City Mall, a lively mall with a great waterfront location and plenty of leisure and entertainment options, you'll find Bowling City.

Located on the balcony level, this centre has 12 hi-tech bowling lanes with various special effects to jazz up the experience, including synchronised coloured lighting and fog and mist effects. For beginners and little ones there are bumpers and ramps available to ensure everyone gets a fair chance, and there are plenty of differently weighted bowling balls to suit all. Also on offer at Bowling City are nine billiard tables, a number of PlayStation booths and a 24-station PC gaming network and a karaoke cabin. So, after you've celebrated making a few strikes, you can take your adrenaline rush into the karaoke room and triumphantly belt out *We Are The Champions*.

There are a few other bowling centres in Dubai that are worth a visit, including Al Nasr Leisureland in Oud Metha (which is licensed), and Dubai Bowling Centre, which has its own league for anyone that gets a taste for the game and wants to turn it into a regular activity.

HIGHLIGHTS

Billiards
PlayStation rooms
Karaoke cabin

NEARBY ATTRACTIONS

For a leisurely lunch after a round of bowling, head to Al Badia Golf Club for a bite to eat at Blades, a restaurant with great views.

"After you've hit the lanes, celebrate in the private karaoke rooms."

SWITCH BOWLING DUBAI

WHERE Ibn Battuta Mall
WHEN Daily, 10am-11pm
HOW MUCH From Dhs.25 per game
TIME SPENT Less than three hours
CONTACT 04 440 5961
WEBSITE switchbowlingdubai.com
MAP p.213

There are many top-notch bowling facilities in the UAE, and a favourite among Dubai's residents is Switch Bowling. It's located at Ibn Battuta Mall, with a huge range of shopping and dining options right on the doorstep, as well as plenty of children's play facilities, a 21-screen cinema and exhibitions on the travels of Ibn Battuta himself.

Set within the Indian Court, Switch Bowling has state-of-the-art lighting and sound effects, and 12 glow-in-the-dark lanes that are served by waiters who bring food and refreshments. The decor is pretty funky too, and there's fun for all the family with professional billiard tables, an internet cyber room and network gaming facilities. You can even make a party of it by spending some time in one of the private karaoke and PlayStation rooms after you've hit the lanes, and enjoying some snacks in the onsite cafe and lounge area.

Other bowling centres worth checking out in Dubai include the enormous Dubai International Bowling Centre at Shabab Club & Century Mall which has 36 lanes, and Funky Lanes at Arabian Centre in Mirdif. The latter runs a daily Ladies Happy Hour offering free bowling for women between 10am and 2pm.

HIGHLIGHTS
Glow-in-the-dark lanes
PlayStation rooms
Private karaoke rooms

NEARBY ATTRACTIONS
Ibn Battuta Mall is bursting with attractions. For a more relaxing activity than bowling, catch a film at the IMAX Grand Cinemas.

"Order food and refreshments to be served at your lanes."

ADVENTURE HQ

WHERE Times Square Center
WHEN Saturday to Wednesday, 10am-10pm. Thursday and Friday, 10am-midnight
HOW MUCH From Dhs.50
TIME SPENT Less than three hours
CONTACT 04 346 6824
WEBSITE adventurehq.ae
MAP p.214

Not only is Adventure HQ the ultimate destination for outdoor enthusiasts to stock up on kit, this fantastic store in Times Square Center also boasts a state-of-the-art climbing wall. The wall is a great place to test out your skills and fitness, race your friends and even take part in one of the store's speed climbing competitions.

If that's not enough, there's also a cable obstacle course for testing your balance (and nerve) and a Chill Chamber where you can pit your cold weather gear against the teeth-chattering -25° temperatures. A team of in-store experts is on hand to offer guidance and advice for all activities.

If you can gather a group of likeminded adventurers, you can book the 90-minute party package where the Adventure Zone will be reserved exclusively for the party, and certified instructors will be on hand to supervise and help out. Prices start at Dhs.95 per person from Sunday to Thursday (the party host doesn't pay), and includes a gift bag. A minimum of 10 people is required for this package.

Once you've had your fill of in-store adventures on the wall, it's easy to spend an afternoon browsing and splurging on everything from swimwear and camping gear to stand-up paddleboards.

HIGHLIGHTS
Climbing wall
Cable obstacle course
Chill Chamber

NEARBY ATTRACTIONS
Times Square Center has a unique ice cafe, Chill Out, which serves hot drinks in sub-zero temperatures – perfect for summer.

"Buy the Adventure Zone Multi Pass and get 10 sessions for Dhs.395."

PLAYNATION

WHERE Mirdif City Centre
WHEN Timings vary
HOW MUCH From Dhs.50
TIME SPENT Less than three hours
CONTACT 04 324 0000
WEBSITE theplaymania.com
MAP p.215

BEST FOR
Families

Mirdif City Centre has no shortage of attractions at its Playnation complex, and one of the most popular is the climbing wall. A favourite among mums and dads with young children, especially at the weekends, this indoor climbing wall has clear colour-coded routes designed for everyone from absolute beginners to intermediate climbers. All of the safety equipment and apparel is provided, and there are instructors on hand to offer their expert guidance.

If you're feeling particularly brave, you could even tackle the Sky Trail, a challenging obstacle course that runs along the ceiling of the mall, 13 metres above the ground. You can access it via the climbing wall or through an automatic belay system. It's not for the fainthearted, requiring balance, coordination and nerves of steel to tower above your fellow shoppers – but it is a lot of fun!

Elsewhere in the Playnation section, there is plenty more to fill your weekends – there's Soccer Circus, a football academy, Yalla! Bowling, and Little Explorers, an edutainment centre for younger kids. iFLY Dubai is an indoor skydiving simulator where you can get a taste of this adrenaline-pumping activity and experience your first freefall.

HIGHLIGHTS
Climbing wall
Sky Trail

NEARBY ATTRACTIONS
Adrenaline junkies should head to iFLY Dubai, an indoor skydiving simulator where the whole family can take part.

"Take climbing lessons, which start at just Dhs.75 per hour."

ZAYED SPORTS CITY ICE RINK

WHERE Zayed Sports City, Al Madina Al Riyadiya
WHEN Timings vary
HOW MUCH Free entry Saturday to Wednesday. Skating fee starts at Dhs.40 for two hours
TIME SPENT Less than three hours
CONTACT 02 403 4333
WEBSITE zsc.ae
MAP p.208

If you want to hang out at the coolest spot in the capital – literally – head to Zayed Sports City Ice Rink. This Olympic-sized rink at Zayed Sports City is the only one of its kind in the UAE capital. As well as hosting various events including ice hockey games and figure skating competitions, it's open to recreational skaters of all ages and abilities; there's also a separate children's area.

Whatever your level of ability, whether you've never laced on some skates or are simply looking to improve your skills, there are coaching sessions available for both individuals and groups. It's a great place to hang

out at the weekend with friends and family and, if you get hooked on skating after the first time, you can make a trip to the ice rink a regular activity by becoming a member, with prices starting at Dhs.950.

It is advisable to call ahead before your visit, as the ice rink is sometimes closed to the public and reserved for ice hockey practice. You should also keep in mind that Thursdays are reserved for ladies only.

Alternatively, if you prefer to enjoy ice skating from the safety of the sidelines, check the Zayed Sports City Ice Rink's schedule for upcoming shows and events.

HIGHLIGHTS
Coaching sessions
Ice hockey games
Figure skating shows

NEARBY ATTRACTIONS
Head to nearby Italian restaurant Figaro's to sample some of their delicious pizza after you've worked up an appetite on the ice.

"Gather some friends and book a group coaching session."

AL AIN MALL ICE RINK

WHERE Al Ain Mall
WHEN Saturday to Wednesday, 10am-10pm. Thursday and Friday, 10am-midnight
HOW MUCH Prices start at Dhs.30
TIME SPENT Less than three hours
CONTACT 03 766 0333
WEBSITE alainmall.com
MAP p.210

The state-of-the-art rink at Al Ain Mall is one of its brightest and best attractions. The ice rink offers figure skating lessons led by highly qualified instructors for children as young as three, as well as teens and adults. There are even lessons in ice hockey for those who've mastered the basics of skating.

Of course, it's not all about the competition – there's also the option to simply visit the rink, lace up your skates and test out your skills on the ice. On weekdays, there are eight sessions lasting 90 minutes each held between 10am and 10pm. On Thursdays and Fridays an additional session is kept open for latecomers from 10.30pm to midnight. It's a great idea for a group activity, and the entry fee is cheaper for groups of 15 or more (Dhs.15 as opposed to Dhs.30 for individuals).

Of course, the ice rink isn't the only attraction on offer in Al Ain Mall. As well as the usual shopping and dining facilities, there's Safari Cars – a miniature traffic city with driving tracks aimed at young kids. Little ones are sure to love getting behind the wheel. Alternatively, there's Candy Castle, a supervised play area where kids can learn and have fun while the grown-ups shop.

HIGHLIGHTS
Figure skating lessons
Ice hockey lessons
Late night skating

NEARBY ATTRACTIONS
Al Ain Mall has plenty of family-friendly attractions including Grand Cinemas, Bowling City and the Action Zone play area.

"The rink hosts ice hockey games and figure skating shows."

DUBAI ICE RINK

WHERE The Dubai Mall, Ground floor
WHEN Timings vary
HOW MUCH From Dhs.55
TIME SPENT Less than three hours
CONTACT 04 448 5111
WEBSITE dubaiicerink.com
MAP p.214

BEST FOR
Summer

On the ground floor of The Dubai Mall you'll find a winter wonderland that's perfect for the cooler months. The Dubai Ice Rink, an Olympic-sized arena, is the largest and newest ice rink in the UAE, and is particularly well suited to family days out. Very young children are really well catered for with the popular 'penguin pals' – cute skating aids designed to help little ones feel safe on the ice that cost just Dhs.30 per hour to hire. There are also Mom and Tots sessions (Dhs.55) held throughout the week.

Regular public sessions take place at various times during the day, which allows skaters of all abilities and levels of experience to hit the ice. If you're hoping to improve your skating skills, check out the learn-to-skate sessions that cover everything from basic skills to trickier turns and jumps. It's a great way to build your confidence.

For Dhs.80 per person, you get unlimited access on Fridays and Saturdays between 11am and 4pm. Plus, in addition to the regular public sessions, the ice rink is transformed into an ice disco every Monday, Thursday, Friday and Saturday (times vary). Skaters can get into the groove with two hours of dazzling lights and music. There's an in-house DJ and, yes, he does take requests.

HIGHLIGHTS
Ice disco
Skating lessons
Penguin pals

NEARBY ATTRACTIONS
There's plenty to keep you entertained elsewhere in the mall, from SEGA Republic to the Dubai Aquarium and Underwater Zoo.

"Take part in a disco on ice session, held throughout the week."

YAS MARINA CIRCUIT

WHERE Yas Island West
WHEN Timings vary
HOW MUCH Prices vary
TIME SPENT Full day
CONTACT 02 659 9800
WEBSITE yasmarinacircuit.com
MAP p.209

Head to the home of the annual Formula 1 Etihad Airways Grand Prix to find out exactly what puts Yas Marina Circuit in pole position. This year-round venue on Yas Island is where petrol-heads can put their driving skills to the test with a high-speed, adrenaline-fueled challenge. There's a wide range of driving experiences on offer: get behind the wheel of a Formula Yas 3000, the closest competitor to an actual Formula 1 car, or opt for the SLS AMG Gullwing and feel like an action hero.

First-timers needn't be afraid – the instructors are encouraging and really know their stuff, while non-drivers can get in on the action with a Passenger Experience in an Aston Martin GT4, for example, or by joining a drag racer in a Chevrolet Camaro. You can even bring your own car for a spin during a Yas Track Day. Plus, more family-friendly Arrive & Drive Karting is available at Yas Kartzone next door.

Supercars aside, a visit to Yas Marina Circuit is a chance to experience a world-famous Formula 1 track. Whatever your lap record, whizzing past empty grandstands under the floodlights at speeds of up to 300km/h, in the tracks of the fastest drivers on the planet, is a truly spine-tingling experience.

HIGHLIGHTS
Formula Yas 3000 Experience
AMG 'Gullwing' Experience
Track days

NEARBY ATTRACTIONS
For more high-speed thrills on Yas Island, check out the rollercoasters at Ferrari World and the waterslides at Yas Waterworld.

"Race your friends around the Yas Kartzone nearby."

SPORTS & LEISURE | Karting & Motorsports

AL AIN RACEWAY INTERNATIONAL KART CIRCUIT

WHERE Nr Al Ain Sportplex, Off Al Khatam St
WHEN Timings vary
HOW MUCH Prices start at Dhs.100
TIME SPENT Less than three hours
CONTACT 03 768 6662
WEBSITE alainraceway.com
MAP p.210

The high-speed thrills of Al Ain Raceway International Kart Circuit are not for the faint-hearted: here, drivers reach speeds in excess of 60kmph as they race around the track.

Al Ain Raceway is open to adrenaline junkies young and old and it's possible to book a private session in advance. Racers are divided into age groups – Cadets (aged seven to 11), Juniors (12 to 15) and Seniors (16 and over) – and you can tear around the track solo or race against a group.

After you've signed up, you'll get suited up and have a safety briefing with the expert instructors. Then it's time to burn rubber around the 1.6km

circuit. Each session lasts 15 minutes and a computer records lap times so visitors can see how they measure up against other drivers. The centre even keeps a record of the fastest lap per month and displays it on their website, so drivers can really earn their bragging rights.

The basic practice sessions cost Dhs.100 for 15 minutes on the Indy Circuit or Dhs.150 on the International Circuit. The circuit is a very popular spot for birthday parties and corporate events, but visitors are also welcome to simply turn up on the day and take advantage of the centre's Arrive & Drive package.

HIGHLIGHTS
Arrive & Drive package
1.6km circuit

NEARBY ATTRACTIONS
After your karting session, treat yourself to an indulgent lunch at the Hilton Al Ain or head to one of the city's parks for a picnic.

"Hit speeds of up to 60kmph as you race around the track."

DUBAI KARTDROME & AUTODROME

WHERE Dubai MotorCity
WHEN Timings vary
HOW MUCH From Dhs.100 plus Dhs.10 annual registration fee
TIME SPENT Half day
CONTACT 04 367 8700
WEBSITE dubaiautodrome.com
MAP p.213

MotorCity is geared up for all manner of automotive fun. Visit this residential suburb of Dubai and you'll feel like you're already on a race track before you even enter the Autodrome or Kartdrome.

At Dubai Kartdrome you get the best of both worlds; there's a 62m indoor circuit to keep cool during the summer, and a 1.2km international standard outdoor track for the cooler winter months. The outdoor track has 17 challenging corners that are sure to test your skills, plus a tunnel and bridge for extra excitement. After a safety briefing, you'll take to your 390cc kart (there are 120cc karts

for kids aged seven years and older) and hit the tarmac. Nothing brings family and friends together like a bit of friendly competition!

If you want to splash the cash a little, head across the road to Dubai Autodrome. Dubai's motorsports home has six different track configurations, including a 5.39km FIA-sanctioned GP circuit, state-of-the-art pit facilities and a 7,000-seat grandstand. There's a whole range of auto experiences to choose from that are sure to get your heart racing, including the opportunity to drive the powerful Audi R8 V10 supercar and F1-style single seaters.

HIGHLIGHTS
390cc karts
120cc kid-friendly karts
1.2km outdoor track

NEARBY ATTRACTIONS
In addition to the restaurants and shopping spots of MotorCity, the autodrome is also close to the picturesque Miracle Garden.

"Have a memorable day with a supercar or F1-style driving experience."

EMIRATES KART ZONE

WHERE Al Wasl Sports Club
WHEN Timings vary
HOW MUCH Prices start at Dhs.120
TIME SPENT Half day
CONTACT 050 426 3424
WEBSITE emirateskartzone.net
MAP p.215

Those with a need for speed will find plenty to enjoy at the Emirates Kart Zone. Operating under the Emirates Motor Sports Federation, there is a huge, state-of-the-art outdoor track. Visitors of all ages can take on a Formula 1-style circuit complete with floodlights, hairpin turns and chicanes, behind the wheel of a powerful kart.

Each kart is powered by two 200cc engines, with a slingshot acceleration speed of 80-120km per hour. There are also professional and junior karts available. Prices start at Dhs.120 per person for a 15-minute Arrive & Drive session, although there are special offers during the year.

Karting is the perfect activity for those with a competitive streak, as you get to race the clock as well as your friends or family. At the end of each session, computerised race results reveal the fastest lap times on a big screen. What's more, Emirates Kart Zone keeps a record of the best lap records for each month and the year overall, so you can see how you measure up against other karting enthusiasts.

Overall, it's a great day out for families with older kids too, although they have to be at least 10 years old to compete. Emirates Kart Zone also hosts birthday parties for children aged 10 to 14.

HIGHLIGHTS
Formula 1-style circuit
Timed race results
State-of-the-art karts

NEARBY ATTRACTIONS
There are food and drinks outlets at the track if you need to grab a bite to eat, as well as table tennis tables for between races.

"Try to earn a spot on Emirates Kart Zone's list of best lap times."

JA JEBEL ALI GOLF RESORT

WHERE Nr Palm Jebel Ali
WHEN 10am-5pm (mini golf)
HOW MUCH Dhs.20 per person, plus
day membership rates
TIME SPENT Full day
CONTACT 04 814 5555
WEBSITE jaresortshotels.com
MAP p.212

When it comes to a bit of healthy competition coupled with some fun in the sun, few activities match up to mini golf. Fortunately, the UAE is blessed with some unique and exciting courses, one of the most recent being that at JA Jebel Ali Golf Resort.

This 18-hole course is already proving extremely popular with children and adults alike, with kid-friendly clubs and brightly coloured golf balls, it's the perfect family activity. The course is surprisingly challenging at times and features a range of obstacles, from awkward bends and jumps to tricky loops and uphill putts.

Prices to putt start at Dhs.20 per person, although you'll have to pay for day membership at JA Jebel Ali Golf Resort on top of that, with rates starting at Dhs.180 for non-members (Dhs.90 for children) from Sunday to Thursday. However, it's well worth it to spend the whole day at this lush, green resort with access to swimming pools and a long private beach from sunrise to sunset.

Those with a more serious interest in teeing off can take on the resort's nine-hole, championship standard golf course which has in the past hosted the European PGA Tour event, the Dubai Desert Classic.

HIGHLIGHTS
Mini golf course
Watersports
Beach & swimming pools

NEARBY ATTRACTIONS
Stay at the resort and try watersports at Watercooled, then cool down with sundowners at the Captain's Bar on the seafront.

"Factor in time to enjoy the swimming pools and private beach."

TEE & PUTT MINI GOLF

WHERE Wafi Mall
WHEN Weekdays, 10am-10pm.
Weekends, 10am-midnight
HOW MUCH Prices start from Dhs.75
TIME SPENT Less than three hours
CONTACT 04 357 3290
WEBSITE teeandputt.com
MAP p.215

For superb indoor entertainment during the hot summer months, you can't go wrong with a trip to Tee & Putt Mini Golf. This fairly recent addition to Wafi Mall, located in the lower level, offers mini golf with a fun twist – all the games take place in a glow-in-the-dark world of UV lights and surreal outer space designs, all set to a lively pop soundtrack.

The premise is simple – choose your putter and glow-in-the-dark golf ball and you're ready to tackle the 18-hole, obstacle-riddled course. There's even a par number set for each hole (normally around three) and scorecards to keep a tally.

The course follows a space theme: you can expect to tap golf balls around meteorites, across craters and past aliens. Although it's suitable for all ages, Tee & Putt caters particularly well for kids (and the young at heart) with opportunities for little ones to paint their own designs onto glow-in-the-dark t-shirts or get their faces painted. The venue also has a space for hosting parties.

Over on the other side of town, in Dubai Marina, you'll find Play A Round @ Some Place Nice (playaround.ae), an indoor nine-hole, par three neon golf room with a cafe and an arts and crafts room.

BEST FOR
Summer

HIGHLIGHTS
Glow-in-the-dark course
Space-themed obstacles
The challenging 18th hole

NEARBY ATTRACTIONS
After you've built up an appetite on the mini golf course, refuel with a spot of lunch at Lebanese restaurant, Wafi Gourmet.

"There's a choice of child and adult-sized putters to suit all ages."

AL FORSAN INTERNATIONAL SPORTS RESORT

WHERE Khalifa City A
WHEN Timings vary
HOW MUCH Prices start at Dhs.55
TIME SPENT Full day
CONTACT 02 556 8555
WEBSITE alforsan.com
MAP p.209

Al Forsan is the ultimate amusement and activity centre: the site offers two themed paintballing fields, clay pigeon shooting and archery, and a superb equestrian centre offering pony rides and riding lessons. Its piece-de-resistance, however, is the world-class cable park where you can try your hand at cableboarding.

Like wakeboarding (or waterskiing) but without the boat, you're pulled along by cable links wired around a lake. It's a good way to start boarding thanks to the calm waters and steady tension on the tow line, especially as one of the lakes at Al Forsan is dedicated entirely to beginners.

Over on the expert lake, boarders and skiers zip their way around, jumping over ramps and practising superhuman tricks. Pro and beginner equipment, including lifejackets and helmets, are provided and staff are more than willing to give tips to get you up and boarding.

The resort also has a motorsports centre, which offers up a range of petrol-powered activities for driving fans. There's the 1.2km CIK-approved circuit with various layouts and vehicles with top speeds of up to 120kmph available; there's also a kids' karting track for children aged eight to 11; and a dual circuit, off-road buggy track.

HIGHLIGHTS
Cableboarding park
Equestrian centre
Motorsports centre

NEARBY ATTRACTIONS
To keep with the motorsports theme, head for either Yas Marina Circuit or Yas Kartzone to burn some rubber.

"If you're new to cableboarding, try the lake for beginners only."

ZAYED SPORTS CITY

WHERE Al Khaleej Al Arabi St,
Al Madina Al Riyadiya
WHEN Timings vary
HOW MUCH Prices vary
(free to cycle the grounds)
TIME SPENT Full day
CONTACT 02 403 4200
WEBSITE zsc.ae
MAP p.208

For an active weekend in Abu Dhabi, Zayed Sports City is, in many ways, the ultimate destination. For one thing, there's the staggering size of the complex – the multipurpose stadium alone has enough space to accommodate up to 43,000 people, and regularly plays host to high profile events from international football to A-list music concerts. Then there's the variety of activities and attractions on offer, and plenty of restaurants and cafes nearby.

Head to the International Tennis Centre, where there are three outdoor hard surface courts – the perfect setting for a game of basketball or netball – or hire one of the beach volleyball courts and bump, set and spike the afternoon away. There are also softball, baseball and football pitches for hire. Alternatively, simply bring your bike and take a leisurely cycle around the grounds for free, or go rollerblading along the pathways.

For something more sedate, you can go bowling at the Khalifa International Bowling Centre or ice-skating at the Zayed Sports City Ice Rink. For tots there's a shaded playground, and for daring teens there's a small skate park. It's the perfect place to hang out with friends and family for a full day of sporting action.

HIGHLIGHTS
Beach volleyball courts
Cycle paths
Ice rink

NEARBY ATTRACTIONS
Relax in Khalifa Park over an alfresco lunch, or soak up some culture with a tour of the iconic Sheikh Zayed Grand Mosque.

"Check the website for details of summer camps for kids."

WADI ADVENTURE

WHERE Off Al Ain Fayda Rd, Jebel Hafeet
WHEN Sunday to Thursday, 11am-10pm. Friday and Saturday, 10am-8pm
HOW MUCH Prices start at Dhs.50
TIME SPENT Full day
CONTACT 03 781 8422
WEBSITE wadiadventure.ae
MAP p.210

BEST FOR
Full day

Wadi Adventure is a typical example of how anything is possible in the UAE – even surfing in the middle of the desert. This water park with a difference is home to a stunning wave pool that generates three-metre high breaks every 90 seconds. Catching a wave against the backdrop of the rugged Hajar Mountains is a surreal experience, to say the least!

You'll also find white water rafting and kayaking runs of more than a kilometre in length. A giant conveyor belt drags you to the summit and then it's up to your own paddle power to complete the course. Beginner rapids are suitable for families, but the higher grades will keep thrill-seekers on their toes. It's harder than it looks, and patient instructors are on hand to maintain a safe and relaxed environment. Lessons are available too, for any visitors who want to sharpen their skills.

If water isn't your thing, the tree-top obstacles of the Air Park, as well as a zip line, climbing wall and canyon swing, should keep your excitement levels vertiginously high. While most of the activities are for older kids and adults, there's a family swimming pool, man-made beach and a splash pool for little ones, making it a fantastic option for a family outing.

HIGHLIGHTS
White water rafting
Zip line from the Air Park
Surf pool

NEARBY ATTRACTIONS
Other family-friendly attractions in the area include the excellent Al Ain Zoo and lush green theme park Hili Fun City.

"Grab a paddle and try the white water rapids and kayaking runs."

AL NASR LEISURELAND

WHERE Oud Metha
WHEN 9am until late
HOW MUCH Prices vary
TIME SPENT Full day
CONTACT 04 337 1234
WEBSITE alnasrll.com
MAP p.215

This large leisure complex is located behind American Hospital in Oud Metha, and has a variety of activities that make for a budget-friendly, family day out. The highlight is an outdoor swimming pool with a wave machine, slides and a baby pool, which costs from just Dhs.40 per person.

After a day spent splashing around, you can head over to the Olympic-size ice rink, strap on a pair of blades and show off your skills, or catch one of the regular ice shows held here. Be sure to call in advance for information and to check the session times, as the rink is sometimes closed for ice hockey practice sessions.

If you're not worn out yet, head to the bowling alley, which has eight lanes and plenty of fast food options, as well as a licensed bar. Also housed in the complex are more bars and restaurants, including Sanjeev Kapoor's specialist Indian eatery, the popular Khazana, which serves up the tastiest option for dinner.

The complex also has squash and tennis courts, arcade games and shops, making it the perfect destination to spend a full day. Once you've had your fill of the amusements on offer, head to Grand Cinemas at Wafi City, buy some popcorn and relax in front of a blockbuster movie.

HIGHLIGHTS
Ice skating
Bowling
Wave pool and slides

NEARBY ATTRACTIONS
Head to the par-72 course at Al Badia Golf Club or drive to Al Fahidi Historical Neighbourhood for a cultural visit.

"Enjoy the outdoor swimming pool during the winter months."

SHARJAH GOLF & SHOOTING CLUB

WHERE Sheikh Mohammed Bin Zayed Rd
WHEN Timings vary
HOW MUCH Prices vary
TIME SPENT Half day
CONTACT 06 548 7777
WEBSITE golfandshootingshj.com
MAP p.219

This snazzy facility on the outskirts of Sharjah has a variety of trigger-happy activities. The shooting range boasts indoor pistols, rifles and revolvers, as well as 25m and 50m ranges, and there's archery equipment for budding Robin Hoods, all with fully trained instructors on hand. For some serious fun, turn your family and friends into your mortal enemies with a game of paintball.

There are two innovative outdoor parks to choose from, including a space that's been made to look like a World War I battlefield, as well as a giant outdoor jungle. Indoors, there's a London-themed battlefield complete with black taxis, red telephone booths and even a Harrods and Ritz Hotel to hide in.

The mission is simple – after you've donned some protective gear (chest plates, neck protectors and masks – safety is taken seriously), aim and fire on the opposition – and once you're in the battle zone, show no mercy.

There are several rounds, each lasting up to 20 minutes, with two referees always on the field to make sure everyone plays by the rules. Once you've got the hang of it, you'll soon be living out your GI Joe fantasies: huddling in corners, discussing tactics and preying on the weak.

HIGHLIGHTS
Glow-in-the-dark night games
London-themed indoor park

NEARBY ATTRACTIONS
After your exertions on the battlefield, take a break in Sharjah National Park or visit the Sharjah Classic Car Museum.

"Airsoft and speedball games are also available at the club."

SKI DUBAI

WHERE Mall of the Emirates
WHEN Sunday to Wednesday, 10am-11pm. Thursday, 10am-midnight. Friday, 9am-midnight, Saturday, 9am-11pm
HOW MUCH Prices vary.
TIME SPENT Full day
CONTACT 04 409 4090
WEBSITE skidxb.com
MAP p.213

BEST FOR
Summer

What do you do when the desert heat is pushing 40 degrees? Ski, of course! Leave the sun, sea and sand outside and head to this winter wonderland, complete with 22,500 square metres of real snow. The temperature hovers around -2°C even when it's closer to 50°C outside, making it perfect for a cool escape.

Competent skiers and boarders can choose between five runs of different difficulty (there's even a black run) and a freestyle area, but skiing and snowboarding lessons are available for beginners on the less steep slopes. There's also a huge Snow Park, where you can take little ones tobogganing,

roll down the Giant Ball run, turn down the tube slides, sightsee in the chairlift, or enjoy a mug of hot chocolate at -3°C. You can even get up close with a colony of snow penguins, who are the stars of a daily show – look into organising a 'Peng Friend Encounter'. Slope passes and lesson prices include the hire charge for jackets, trousers, boots, socks, helmets – and either skis and poles or a snowboard – but it's worth bringing your own gloves as you'll be charged extra for these.

For all round family fun, consider getting a Playmania gift card - a pre-loaded card that can be used at Ski Dubai, iFLY Dubai and Magic Planet.

HIGHLIGHTS
Black run
Tobogganing hills
Zorbing in the Giant Ball

NEARBY ATTRACTIONS
The Mall of the Emirates is packed with fun attractions, including VOX Cinemas and amusement arcade, Magic Planet.

"Time your visit to catch the daily March of the Penguins show."

iFLY DUBAI

WHERE Mirdif City Centre
WHEN Sunday to Wednesday, 10am-11pm. Thursday to Saturday, 10am-midnight
HOW MUCH Prices start at Dhs.215
TIME SPENT Less than three hours
CONTACT 04 231 6292
WEBSITE theplaymania.com
MAP p.215

If you like the idea of a skydive but don't have the budget (or the head for heights), visit iFLY at Playnation, where you can try some gravity-defying indoor 'skydiving'. Not only is it much more wallet-friendly than jumping out of a plane, this activity is suitable for the whole family (the minimum age is three years old). What's more, the free fall feeling lasts longer than it would during a real skydive.

Giant vertical wind tunnels simulate the sensation of jumping from a plane – you hover over powerful fans while being blasted as high as 10 metres in the air by winds of up to 200kmph. Do note that there are some weight and height restrictions, so check the website before you visit.

Even seasoned skydivers have been known to visit iFLY for the longer 'free fall'. While the feeling of weightlessness is similar to that of skydiving, the 'floating' sensation is more like that of flying, making for an exhilarating experience. It may sound scary, but fear not – for first timers, there are experienced instructors on hand to help, and visitors as young as three can take part. There's also the option to buy souvenir DVDs and photos to capture the (sometimes hilarious) reaction to the experience as a unique memento.

HIGHLIGHTS
Longer 'free fall'
Souvenir DVDs and photos

NEARBY ATTRACTIONS
Mirdif City Centre is packed with fun attractions, from arcade games at Magic Planet to the lanes at Yalla! Bowling.

"Children as young as three can try iFLY, so take the whole family."

WATERCOOLED

WHERE JA Jebel Ali Golf Resort
WHEN Daily, 9:30am-7pm
Bookings necessary
HOW MUCH Prices vary
TIME SPENT Half day
CONTACT 04 887 6771
WEBSITE watercooleddubai.com
MAP p.212

Based at JA Jebel Ali Golf Resort, Watercooled has a wide range of affordable watersports on offer – especially as you don't even have to pay entrance to the resort before using the centre's facilities. There's a sheltered bay, which means the water is calm and flat, no matter what the weather – perfect for adrenaline sports such as wakeboarding, waterskiing, kitesurfing, windsurfing and more, as well as super-fun inflatable tow rides.

You can also try more sedate activities such as stand up paddleboarding and kayaking, and the centre offers a variety of RYA (Royal Yachting Association) courses, from powerboating to dinghy sailing. The clubhouse, which is located right on the beach, is a welcoming open-plan wooden chalet with decking and loungers. You can even watch your performance on the water courtesy of GoPro cameras that capture your day, and there's complimentary water, towels and wifi for visitors.

All the equipment here is superb; the boats are powerful and top of the range. The experienced and passionate instructors are all fully qualified to teach to international standards, and they're always on hand to guide newbies and help improve the technique of more experienced guests.

HIGHLIGHTS
Kitesurfing
Donut rides
Waterskiing

NEARBY ATTRACTIONS
Make a day of it at the resort and swing into action on the nine-hole golf course or go horse-riding in the paddock.

"Test your stamina (and bravery) on a thrilling zapcat ride."

UMM AL QUWAIN MARINE CLUB

WHERE Nr Palm Beach Resort
WHEN Timings vary
HOW MUCH Prices start at Dhs.35
TIME SPENT Full day
CONTACT 06 766 6644
WEBSITE uaqmarineclub.com
MAP p.217

Umm Al Quwain's placid lagoon provides a wonderfully calm and safe environment for watersports such as wakeboarding, windsurfing and banana boating. UAQ Marine Club runs all of these activities and more, and at extremely competitive prices – from Dhs.35 for one hour's kayak rental. The club also runs cruises through the mangroves on a boat that's available for hire. Open sides allow good viewing of the resident flamingos and their habitat, and the waterslide is great fun. Other boats are available for deep sea fishing trips.

You can spend the day here using the facilities – there's a large swimming pool and a children's play area, as well as two restaurants. There are also areas to play volleyball, table tennis and football.

Situated on the inner reaches of the peninsula that protects Umm Al Quwain's calm waters from the open sea, the club is less than an hour's drive from Dubai and the northern emirates. There's no need to pay for a pricey membership and you don't even need to be an overnight guest, although it's best to book ahead.

While Umm Al Quwain Marine Club is perfect for a day trip, there's the option to extend your stay by camping on the beach.

HIGHLIGHTS
Turtles and flamingos
Kayaking

NEARBY ATTRACTIONS
Umm Al Quwain is best known for its natural beauty, but its man-made attractions include Dreamland Aqua Park.

"Enjoy a slow boat cruise through the peaceful mangroves."

DUBAI
DOLPHINARIUM

Dolphin & Seal Show
Mon to Sat - 11am & 6pm
Fri & Sat - 11am, 3pm & 6pm

Swimming with Dolphins
Mon to Thu - 1pm to 4pm

Swim with our Dolphins

For Details & Tickets Visit www.dubaidolphinarium.ae

Location: Creek Park, Gate 1, Dubai, Call: +971 4 336 9773, Toll Free: 800-DOLPHIN (800-3657446)

Our Vision: To create an excellent city that provides the essence of success and comfort of living.

Wildlife & Sealife

DUBAI AQUARIUM & UNDERWATER ZOO

WHERE The Dubai Mall
WHEN Timings vary
HOW MUCH Tunnel and zoo combo ticket: Dhs.70 (adult), Dhs.55 (children). Dive packages start at Dhs.290
TIME SPENT Less than three hours
CONTACT 04 448 5200
WEBSITE thedubaiaquarium.com
MAP p.214

Located somewhat bizarrely in the middle of The Dubai Mall, this aquarium displays over 33,000 tropical fish to passing shoppers free of charge. For a closer view of the main tank's inhabitants, which include fearsome looking sand tiger sharks, you can pay to walk through the 270° viewing tunnel.

If you've ever gazed into the glass panels of the aquarium and longed to swim with the sharks and exotic fish, you can go for a scuba dive in the tank (call ahead to book). You'll come face to face with some seriously scary predators and a staggering array of fish species – and even feel like a celebrity as hundreds of faces peer at you from the mall. For those who don't fancy being eyed up as potential shark bait, you can keep your distance with a cage snorkel experience, or a ride in a glass-bottomed boat at the Underwater Zoo, located on Level 2.

Well worth a visit, the zoo is popular with kids, and home to some super cute residents such as Gentoo penguins in their own sub-zero habitat, plus otters, beavers, crocodiles, giant spider crabs and seahorses. You can look through a glass floor into the aquarium, or brave the rope bridge in the rainforest section – watch out for creepy crawlies!

HIGHLIGHTS
Underwater viewing tunnel
Glass-bottomed boat ride
Penguin enclosure

NEARBY ATTRACTIONS
Visit the 124th floor of the Burj Khalifa, get your thrills at SEGA Republic and dine out at The Cheesecake Factory.

"Jump into this gigantic fish bowl and go scuba diving with the sharks."

DUBAI DOLPHINARIUM

WHERE Creek Park, Gate 1

WHEN Monday to Thursday, 11am and 6pm. Friday and Saturday, 11am, 3pm and 6pm.

HOW MUCH Dolphin & Seal Show from Dhs.50 (child). Swimming with dolphins from Dhs.550

TIME SPENT Less than three hours

CONTACT 04 336 9773

WEBSITE dubaidolphinarium.ae

MAP p.215

Splashing about with Flipper is surely every child's fantasy, and on many an adult's secret bucket list. For a day that's absolutely guaranteed to delight the kids, head over to Dubai Dolphinarium and meet these friendly and fascinating creatures.

The Dolphinarium has proved to be a popular addition to Creek Park and the main attraction is the seal and dolphin show, which runs twice a day during the week, and three times daily at weekends. During the show you will meet the resident bottlenose dolphins and northern fur seals, who perform some impressive stunts set to music, lights and lasers. Afterwards,

you can have your picture taken with them, or even jump in for playtime. In the water you can grab onto a firm fin and be taken for an exhilarating ride, whizzing across the pool at a surprisingly powerful speed. Getting a close up, pearly grin from one of these awe-inspiring animals is a pretty special experience.

The Dolphinarium has additional attractions, including a Mirror Maze where the kids can play, and a 5D cinema with some wacky special effects for an immersive cinematic experience. There's also the UAE's only exotic bird show – an action-packed, interactive event.

HIGHLIGHTS
Dolphin & Seal Show
5D cinema
Exotic bird show

NEARBY ATTRACTIONS
Relax at Creek Park with a picnic, head to Dubai Festival City Mall for some shopping, or soak up some culture at Dubai Museum.

"For Dhs.550, visitors can go swimming with the dolphins."

THE LOST CHAMBERS AQUARIUM

WHERE Atlantis, The Palm
WHEN Daily, 10am-10pm
HOW MUCH UAE resident rates
Dhs.75 (adults), Dhs.50 (children)
TIME SPENT Half day
CONTACT 04 426 1040
WEBSITE atlantisthepalm.com
MAP p.213

BEST FOR
Families

The ruins of the mysterious, lost underwater city provide the theme for this enormous aquarium at Atlantis, The Palm. A maze of underwater halls and tunnels provide ample opportunity to get up close to the aquarium's 65,000 inhabitants, ranging from sharks and eels to rays and piranhas, as well as a multitude of tropical fish.

While you can see quite a lot from the hotel windows as a guest, it is well worth splashing out for the views inside. For an insight into the aquarium's residents, join one of the hourly guided tours. There's also a twice-daily show with divers in the striking Seven Sage Chamber (home to some giant catfish), and the fish-feeding sessions in the Ambassador Lagoon bring you face to face with sharks, stingrays and smaller fish in a feeding frenzy.

Other activities on offer (at extra cost) include a behind-the-scenes tour, with a visit to the fish hospital and a chance to feed the sealife.

If you're feeling adventurous, the Ultimate Snorkel and Ultimate Dive experiences at the Ambassador Lagoon get daring swimmers even closer to the sharks, rays and colourful reef fish. Both fun and educational, this is a truly interactive experience.

HIGHLIGHTS
Guided tours
Ultimate Snorkel experience
Seven Sage Chamber

NEARBY ATTRACTIONS
Frolic with dolphins at Dolphin Bay or enjoy the thrilling rides at Aquaventure. Round off the day by dining at Locatelli's.

"See sharks, rays and fish being fed in the Ambassador Lagoon."

SHARJAH AQUARIUM

WHERE Al Khan Historical Area
WHEN Saturday, Monday to Thursday, 8am-8pm. Friday, 4pm-10pm
HOW MUCH Dhs.20 (adults) Dhs.10 (children, six-15 years)
TIME SPENT Less than three hours
CONTACT 06 528 5288
WEBSITE sharjahaquarium.ae
MAP p.218

As with many of Sharjah's superb museums and attractions, the priority at this aquarium is education and this, along with the modest entry fee, is the major draw here. There are 250 species on display, with particular attention paid to the species found in the Gulf and the reefs off Sharjah's east coast enclaves, including clownfish, seahorses, turtles, rays and reef sharks.

Along with informative and colourful displays of these beautiful sea creatures, there's a chance to learn about the unique habitats native to the UAE. The town of Kalba, for example, is home to the world's northernmost mangroves and you'll be surprised to find out about the biodiversity found here, both above and below the waves.

Back on land, quirky decor that nods to Sharjah's maritime heritage lends a quaint, down-to-earth feel that, along with the lack of crowds, make this a pleasant place to spend time – arguably more so than some of the UAE's glitzier attractions. There's a great cafe onsite with outdoor seating overlooking the serene Al Khan Lagoon, and an interesting gift shop. Tickets to the aquarium include entrance to the neighbouring Sharjah Maritime Museum, which is well worth having a look around.

HIGHLIGHTS
Reef sharks
Sea turtles

NEARBY ATTRACTIONS
Pop next door to Sharjah Maritime Museum, then head to Al Qasba for a trip on the Eye of the Emirates ferris wheel.

"Dine at the cafe overlooking the fishing boats on the lagoon."

ABU DHABI FALCON HOSPITAL

WHERE Off Sweihan Rd, Al Shamkha
WHEN Sunday to Thursday, 10am-2pm. Tours can be booked in advance
HOW MUCH Dhs.170
TIME SPENT Less than three hours
CONTACT 02 575 5155
WEBSITE falconhospital.com
MAP p.209

The falcon is one of the most revered animals in Arabia and a proud symbol of the nation's heritage. Today, the traditional sport of falconry is still practised throughout the Gulf and one of the best ways to learn more about this fascinating pastime is by taking a trip to the Abu Dhabi Falcon Hospital.

The hospital is the largest of its kind in the world. During a two-hour tour of the hospital, visitors can gain an insight into the history of falconry and the role that this prestigious sport continues to play. There is a lot of emphasis on interaction, and you'll get a chance to get close to the falcons and chat to their handlers.

While you're here, be sure to check out some of the other facilities. You could take your dog for obedience training and exercise at the pet care centre's dog agility park. Alternatively, head to the Royal Grooming Parlour for some pet pampering.

There's a Saluki Centre nearby where you can meet some purebred saluki dogs that are inherent to Bedouin culture (you'll need to prearrange your visit). The centre breeds and trains them as hunting dogs, and offers advice to owners. Looking for a pet? Visit the nearby Abu Dhabi Animal Shelter to see if there are any furry friends that need a home.

HIGHLIGHTS
Hospital guided tour
Owl aviary

NEARBY ATTRACTIONS
Prearrange a visit to the Saluki Centre, where you can see the purebred saluki dogs that are native to Bedouin culture.

"Take a guided tour to learn about this illustrious sport."

EMIRATES PARK ZOO

WHERE Al Bahya
WHEN Weekdays, 9:30am-8pm
Weekends, 9:30am-9pm
HOW MUCH Dhs.25 (adults)
Dhs.10 (children)
TIME SPENT Full day
CONTACT 02 563 3100
WEBSITE emiratesparkzoo.com
MAP p.209

Just half an hour's drive from Dubai lies one of the UAE's most popular family-friendly attractions. The newly renovated Emirates Park Zoo is home to nearly 2,000 species of animal with a number of interactive attractions to help visitors young and old get close to their favourite furry, finned and feathered friends.

Across five acres, you'll find everything from formidable predators such as lions, bears and rare white tigers to herds of camels, ibex and ostrich as well as reptiles, tropical fish and more domesticated creatures too. There's also a flamingo park, where you can spot large exotic birds, including one of the zoo's most recent additions: the great white pelican.

The emphasis at Emirates Park Zoo is on combining learning and fun with hands-on experiences that allow visitors to get close to the animals. At the Giraffe Cafe kids get the thrill of feeding these long-necked (and long-tongued) friendly mammals. You can pet goats, sheep and other farm animals or, if you're brave enough, pose for a picture with a python.

Younger visitors can even volunteer to work as a 'zoo keeper' and learn how the animals are looked after. Watch this space for news of hippos, sealions and anacondas.

HIGHLIGHTS
Giraffe Cafe
Predator park
Sealion shows

NEARBY ATTRACTIONS
Grab some lunch at the nearby Emirates Park Resort and let the kids run free in the jungle gyms at Funscape.

> "Make sure you catch a glimpse of the rare white tigers."

AL AIN ZOO

WHERE Nhayyan Al Awwal St
WHEN Timings vary
HOW MUCH Dhs.15 (adults)
Dhs.5 (children)
TIME SPENT Full day
CONTACT 03 799 2000
WEBSITE alainzoo.ae
MAP p.210

BEST FOR
Families

Al Ain Zoo is the perfect place for a family day out, with plenty to entertain both kids and grown-ups. Thankfully, the zoo is not characterised by small cages and meagre wildlife displays. Instead, it feels much more like a safari park, with spacious enclosures spread across its 900 acres interspersed with other, smaller exhibitions. You'll find everything from zebras roaming wide open spaces to orangutans and chimpanzees playing in their enclosures.

Highlights include watching the hippos splash around in their 10m-long ravine, catching a glimpse of the rare white lions, and getting up close to the giraffes at their feeding station, where Dhs.30 will buy you a cup of carrots.

At the entrance booth, not only can you buy your cheap-as-chips tickets, but you can also purchase the service of a golf buggy and driver to chaperone you through the park.

It might sound like a lazy option, but the zoo is huge, so it's a great little add-on during the hotter months. You can hop on and off, and it's even possible to hail a buggy if you start to get tired. When it's time to take a break, there are also plenty of shaded areas, a new children's playground, daily keeper talks, a cafe and kiosks across the park.

HIGHLIGHTS
Giraffe feeding station
Baby hippos
Parrot show

NEARBY ATTRACTIONS
For a full family day out, combine a trip to Al Ain Zoo with a visit to the ever-entertaining theme park, Hili Fun City.

"Be sure to catch the falcons and eagles at the daily bird show."

AL TAMIMI STABLES

WHERE Nr Al Zubair Municipality, Al Zubair
WHEN Daily, 2pm-10pm
HOW MUCH Dhs.60 (adults), Dhs.35 (children). Activities cost extra
TIME SPENT Full day
CONTACT 06 743 1122
WEBSITE tamimistables.com
MAP p.219

It's not often that you'll see ostriches and oryx, goats and gazelles, rabbits and reindeer all in one place – but Al Tamimi Stables is a spacious farm that's home to over 500 exotic and domestic animals.

Spread across 30 acres, this outdoor venue is a hidden gem for wildlife lovers – or simply a pleasant, green spot for an afternoon stroll. There are pony rides, falcon shows, equestrian displays and guided nature trails, all making for the perfect family day out. Kids can meet, pet and groom cute farm animals in the petting zoo, where you'll find hamsters, baby goats and colourful parrots and cockatoos. There's also the opportunity to learn how the farm works, from planting and harvesting through to food preparation.

Al Tamimi is a professional working stable with breeds including Arabian, Andalusian and Shetland ponies – and there's often a chance to see the horses being fed, trained or groomed.

Nature aside, there's ample room to burn off some energy here, with a choice of tennis courts, football and cricket pitches, and fencing facilities. For a bit of creative downtime, there is a fantastic arts centre where kids of all ages can sign up for classes and workshops.

HIGHLIGHTS
Nature trails
Pony rides
Falcon shows

NEARBY ATTRACTIONS
For a taste of culture, visit the Sharjah Natural History Museum. Or, for a more active day, head for the Sharjah Golf & Shooting Club.

"Look out for the family fun day that takes place around September."

ARABIA'S WILDLIFE CENTRE

WHERE Sharjah Desert Park
WHEN Timings vary
HOW MUCH Dhs.15. Children under 12 go free
TIME SPENT Full day
CONTACT 06 531 1999
WEBSITE epaashj.com
MAP p.219

BEST FOR
Families

Just a short drive from Sharjah, and within easy reach of Sheikh Mohammed Bin Zayed Road, this quality zoo is one of the UAE's best in terms of animal care and presentation. Part of the Sharjah Desert Park complex, be sure to combine it with a visit to Sharjah Natural History & Botanical Museum and the neighbouring Children's Farm.

You won't find the usual zoo suspects such as lions or giraffes at Arabia's Wildlife Centre – home to animals indigenous to the Arabia Peninsula. What you will find, however, is an incredible array of desert species, from the tiny, kangaroo-like lesser

jerboa to the deadly cobra, as well as hyenas, baboons, cheetahs, and even the rare Arabian leopard.

The cafe serves up homemade curries as well as the usual fast food and snacks. It overlooks a beautifully landscaped area of rocks, palms, streams and waterfalls, where oryx, ibex, flamingos and other graceful creatures mill around happily.

Over at the Children's Farm, which is really more of a petting zoo, you can get up close and personal with some familiar faces, including camels and goats. Entrance to the Desert Park covers all three attractions within it.

HIGHLIGHTS
Rare Arabian leopard
Cheetahs
Children's Farm

NEARBY ATTRACTIONS
Combine your visit to the wildlife centre with a trip to the fascinating Sharjah Natural History & Botanical Museum.

"Admire the local birdlife in the walk-through aviary."

Reading a good book is like taking a journey

Your fondest memories are probably the ones where you've curled up with a good book and lost yourself in its world. For children, a book is more than just a tool, it is a gateway to a magical place where learning and wonderment go hand in hand. Give your child the perfect start in life with our excellent selection of childrens' books.

Maps

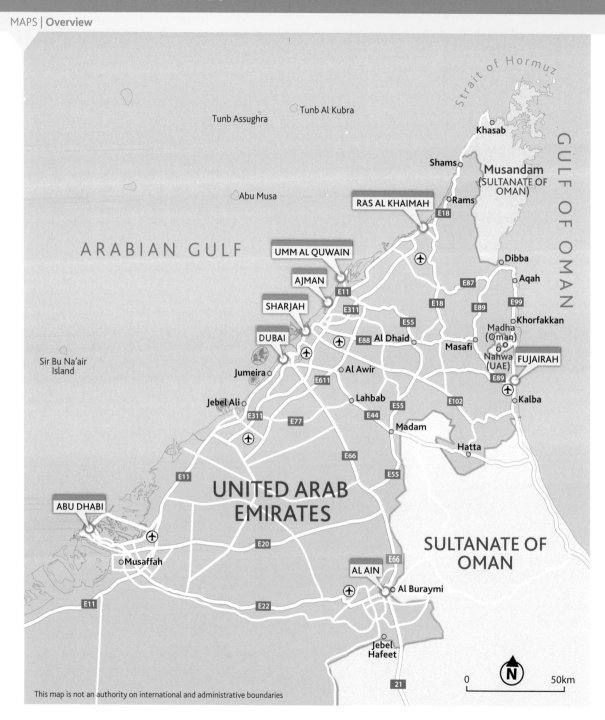

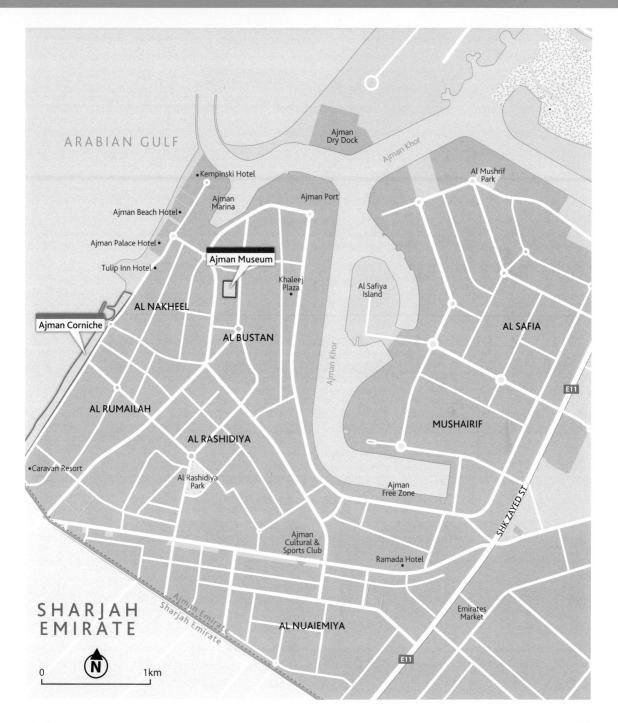

ARABIAN GULF

Ajman Dry Dock

Ajman Khor

Al Mushrif Park

• Kempinski Hotel

Ajman Marina

Ajman Port

Ajman Beach Hotel •

Ajman Palace Hotel •

Ajman Museum

Tulip Inn Hotel •

Khaleej Plaza

Al Safiya Island

AL SAFIA

AL NAKHEEL

Ajman Corniche

AL BUSTAN

Ajman Khor

AL RUMAILAH

MUSHAIRIF

AL RASHIDIYA

E11

• Caravan Resort

Al Rashidiya Park

Ajman Free Zone

SHK ZAYED ST

Ajman Cultural & Sports Club

Ramada Hotel •

Emirates Market

SHARJAH EMIRATE

Ajman Emirate
Sharjah Emirate

AL NUAIEMIYA

E11

0   N   1km

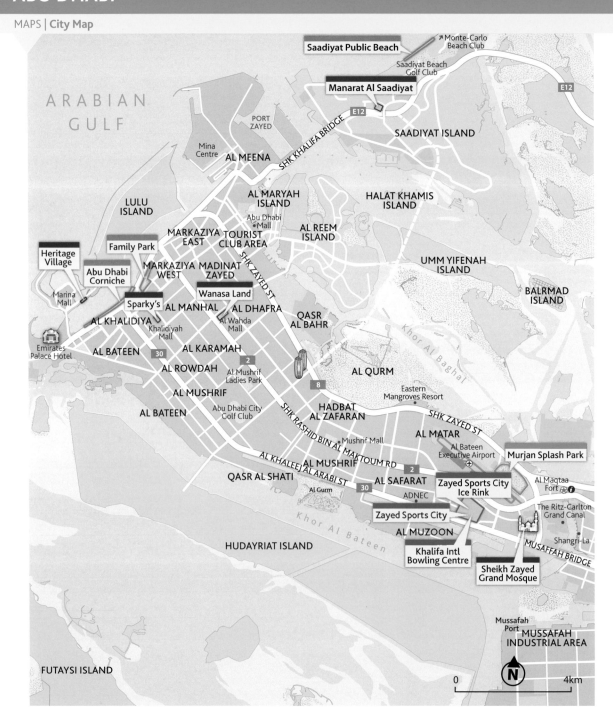

ARABIAN
GULF

PORT
ZAYED

Mina
Centre

AL MEENA

SHK KHALIFA BRIDGE

E12

SAADIYAT ISLAND

Saadiyat Public Beach

Monte-Carlo
Beach Club

Saadiyat Beach
Golf Club

Manarat Al Saadiyat

E12

LULU
ISLAND

AL MARYAH
ISLAND

HALAT KHAMIS
ISLAND

Heritage
Village

Family Park

MARKAZIYA
EAST

Abu Dhabi
Mall

TOURIST
CLUB AREA

AL REEM
ISLAND

UMM YIFENAH
ISLAND

BALRMAD
ISLAND

Abu Dhabi
Corniche

Marina
Mall

MARKAZIYA
WEST

MADINAT
ZAYED

Wanasa Land

SHK ZAYED ST

Sparky's

AL MANHAL

AL DHAFRA

AL KHALIDIYA

AL MANHAL

Al Wahda
Mall

QASR
AL BAHR

Khor Al Baghal

Khalidiyah
Mall

Emirates
Palace Hotel

AL BATEEN

30

AL KARAMAH

2

AL ROWDAH

Al Mushrif
Ladies Park

8

AL QURM

AL MUSHRIF

AL BATEEN

Abu Dhabi City
Golf Club

HADBAT
AL ZAFARAN

Eastern
Mangroves Resort

SHK ZAYED ST

QASR AL SHATI

AL KHALEEJ AL ARABI ST

Al Gurm

SHK RASHID BIN AL MAKTOUM RD

AL MUSHRIF

Mushrif Mall

AL MATAR

Al Bateen
Executive Airport

Murjan Splash Park

Al Maqtaa
Fort

AL SAFARAT

2

30

ADNEC

Zayed Sports City
Ice Rink

Zayed Sports City

The Ritz-Carlton
Grand Canal

Shangri-La

Khor Al Bateen

HUDAYRIAT ISLAND

AL MUZOON

Khalifa Intl
Bowling Centre

Sheikh Zayed
Grand Mosque

MUSAFFAH BRIDGE

Mussafah
Port

MUSSAFAH
INDUSTRIAL AREA

FUTAYSI ISLAND

0   4km

N

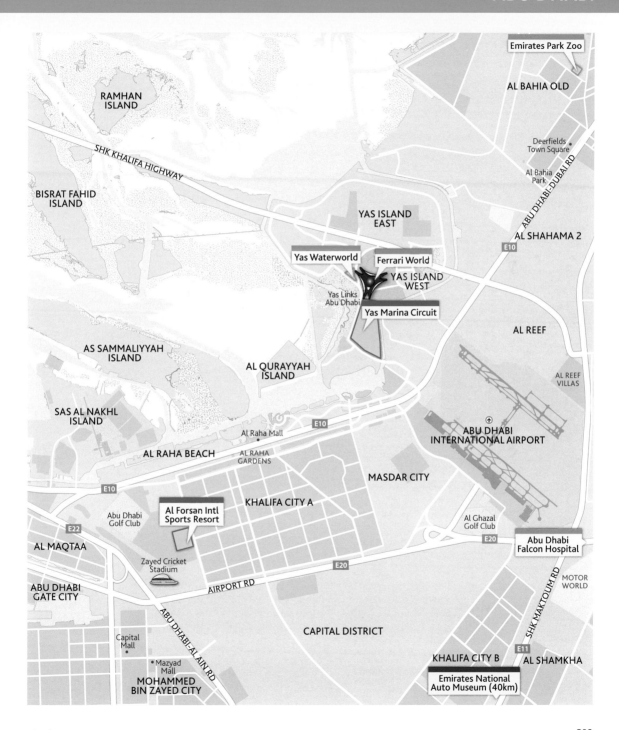

RAMHAN ISLAND

BISRAT FAHID ISLAND

SHK KHALIFA HIGHWAY

Emirates Park Zoo

AL BAHIA OLD

Deerfields Town Square

Al Bahia Park

ABU DHABI-DUBAI RD

YAS ISLAND EAST

AL SHAHAMA 2

E10

Yas Waterworld

Ferrari World

YAS ISLAND WEST

Yas Links Abu Dhabi

AL REEF

Yas Marina Circuit

AS SAMMALIYYAH ISLAND

AL QURAYYAH ISLAND

AL REEF VILLAS

SAS AL NAKHL ISLAND

Al Raha Mall

E10

ABU DHABI INTERNATIONAL AIRPORT

AL RAHA BEACH

AL RAHA GARDENS

MASDAR CITY

E10

Abu Dhabi Golf Club

Al Forsan Intl Sports Resort

KHALIFA CITY A

E22

Al Ghazal Golf Club

Abu Dhabi Falcon Hospital

AL MAQTAA

Zayed Cricket Stadium

E20

E20

ABU DHABI GATE CITY

AIRPORT RD

MOTOR WORLD

Capital Mall

CAPITAL DISTRICT

ABU DHABI-AL AIN RD

SHK MAKTOUM RD

Mazyad Mall

E11

KHALIFA CITY B

AL SHAMKHA

MOHAMMED BIN ZAYED CITY

Emirates National Auto Museum (40km)

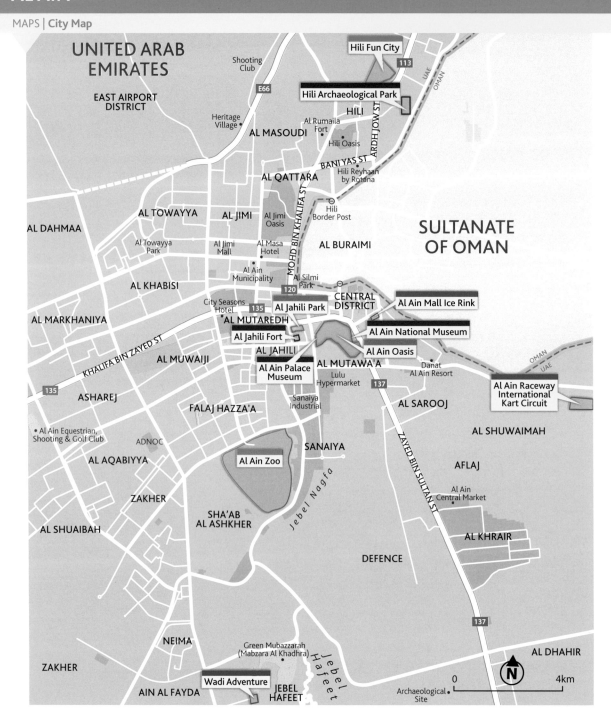

UNITED ARAB
EMIRATES

Shooting
Club

Hili Fun City

113

Hili Archaeological Park

EAST AIRPORT
DISTRICT

E66

HILI

Heritage
Village

Al Rumaila
Fort

AL MASOUDI

Hili Oasis

BANIYAS ST

Hili Reyhaan
by Rotana

ARDH JOWST

UAE

OMAN

AL QATTARA

MOHD BIN KHALIFA ST

AL DAHMAA

AL TOWAYYA

AL JIMI

Al Jimi
Oasis

Hili
Border Post

SULTANATE
OF OMAN

Al Towayya
Park

Al Jimi
Mall

Al Masa
Hotel

AL BURAIMI

Al Ain
Municipality

Al Silmi
Park

AL KHABISI

City Seasons
Hotel

135

Al Jahili Park

120

CENTRAL
DISTRICT

Al Ain Mall Ice Rink

AL MARKHANIYA

AL MUTAREDH

Al Jahili Fort

AL JAHILI

Al Ain National Museum

Al Ain Oasis

AL MUWAIJI

Al Ain Palace
Museum

AL MUTAWA'A

Lulu
Hypermarket

Danat
Al Ain Resort

KHALIFA BIN ZAYED ST

137

AL SAROOJ

Al Ain Raceway
International
Kart Circuit

135

ASHAREJ

FALAJ HAZZA'A

Sanaiya
Industrial

AL SHUWAIMAH

• Al Ain Equestrian,
Shooting & Golf Club

ADNOC

SANAIYA

AFLAJ

ZAYED BIN SULTAN ST

AL AQABIYYA

Al Ain Zoo

Al Ain
Central Market

ZAKHER

Jebel Nagfa

AL KHRAIR

AL SHUAIBAH

SHA'AB
AL ASHKHER

DEFENCE

137

NEIMA

Green Mubazzarah
(Mabzara Al Khadhra)

Jebel Hafeet

AL DHAHIR

ZAKHER

Wadi Adventure

JEBEL
HAFEET

Jebel Hafeet

Archaeological •
Site

0   4km

N

AIN AL FAYDA

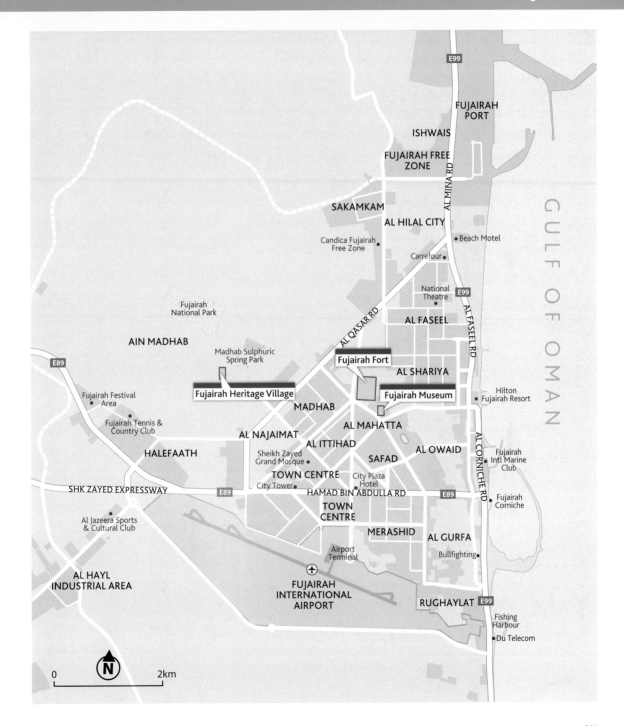

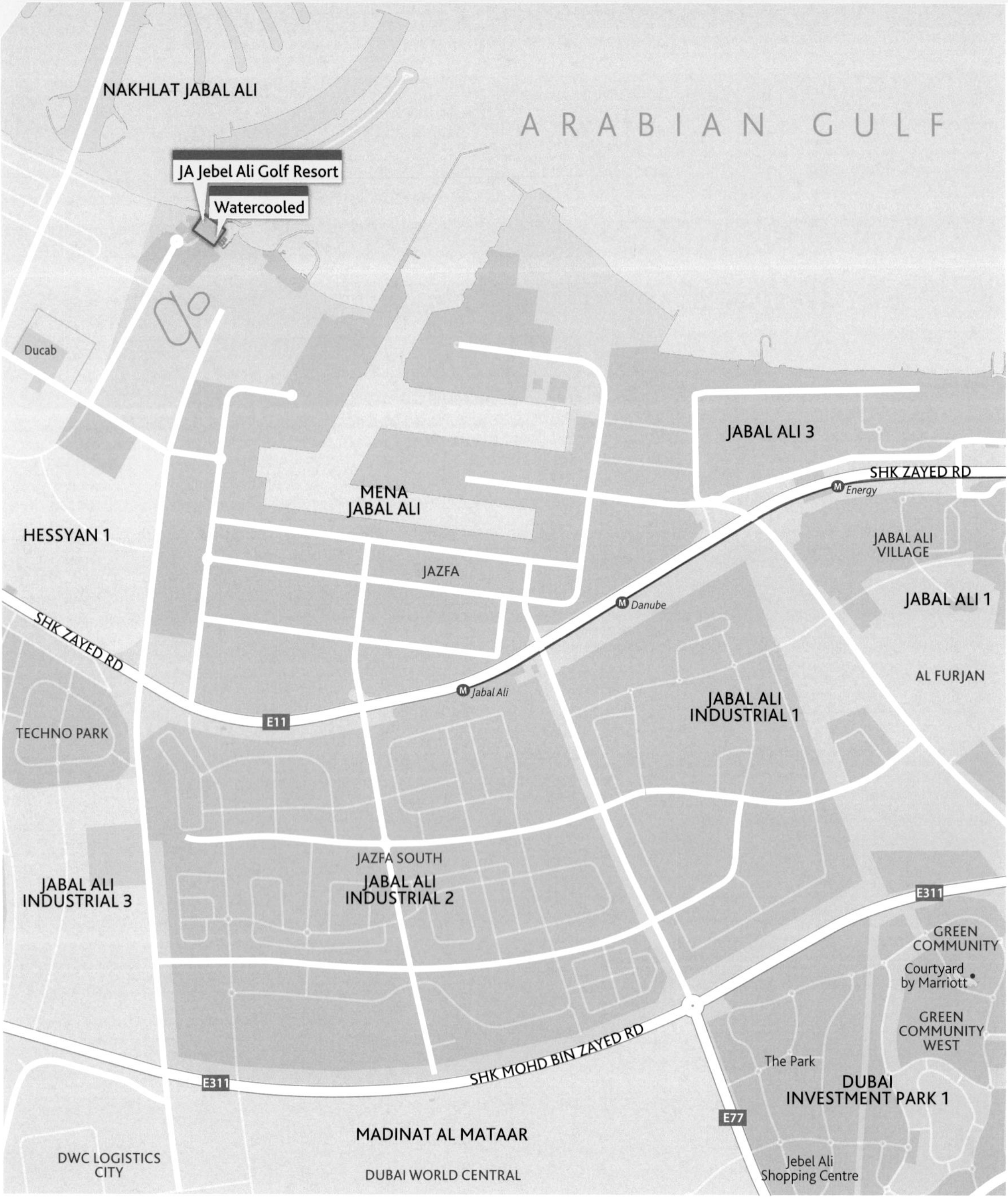

NAKHLAT JABAL ALI

A R A B I A N   G U L F

JA Jebel Ali Golf Resort

Watercooled

Ducab

JABAL ALI 3

SHK ZAYED RD

M *Energy*

MENA
JABAL ALI

HESSYAN 1

JABAL ALI
VILLAGE

JAZFA

JABAL ALI 1

M *Danube*

SHK ZAYED RD

AL FURJAN

M *Jabal Ali*

E11

JABAL ALI
INDUSTRIAL 1

TECHNO PARK

E311

GREEN
COMMUNITY

JAZFA SOUTH

Courtyard
by Marriott

JABAL ALI
INDUSTRIAL 2

JABAL ALI
INDUSTRIAL 3

GREEN
COMMUNITY
WEST

The Park

**DUBAI
INVESTMENT PARK 1**

E311

SHK MOHD BIN ZAYED RD

E77

MADINAT AL MATAAR

Jebel Ali
Shopping Centre

DWC LOGISTICS
CITY

DUBAI WORLD CENTRAL

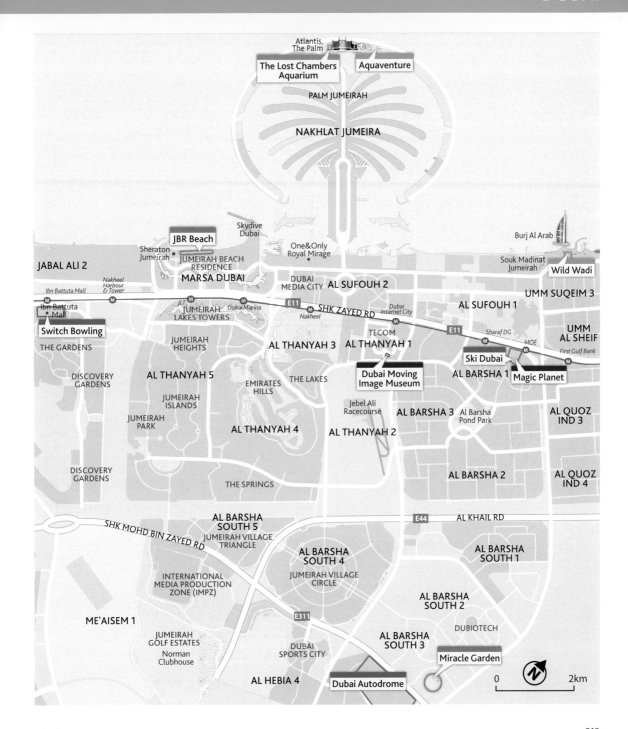

Atlantis,
The Palm

The Lost Chambers
Aquarium

Aquaventure

PALM JUMEIRAH

NAKHLAT JUMEIRA

Skydive
Dubai

Burj Al Arab

JBR Beach

Sheraton
Jumeirah

One&Only
Royal Mirage

Souk Madinat
Jumeirah

JABAL ALI 2

JUMEIRAH BEACH
RESIDENCE

MARSA DUBAI

DUBAI
MEDIA CITY

AL SUFOUH 2

Wild Wadi

UMM SUQEIM 3

Ibn Battuta Mall

Nakheel
Harbour
& Tower

JLT

JUMEIRAH
LAKES TOWERS

Dubai Marina

Nakheel

E11

SHK ZAYED RD

Dubai
Internet City

AL SUFOUH 1

Ibn Battuta
Mall

Switch Bowling

THE GARDENS

JUMEIRAH
HEIGHTS

TECOM

E11

Sharaf DG

MOE

UMM
AL SHEIF

First Gulf Bank

DISCOVERY
GARDENS

AL THANYAH 5

JUMEIRAH
ISLANDS

EMIRATES
HILLS

THE LAKES

AL THANYAH 3

AL THANYAH 1

Dubai Moving
Image Museum

Ski Dubai

AL BARSHA 1

Magic Planet

JUMEIRAH
PARK

AL THANYAH 4

AL THANYAH 2

Jebel Ali
Racecourse

AL BARSHA 3

Al Barsha
Pond Park

AL QUOZ
IND 3

DISCOVERY
GARDENS

THE SPRINGS

AL BARSHA 2

AL QUOZ
IND 4

SHK MOHD BIN ZAYED RD

AL BARSHA
SOUTH 5

JUMEIRAH VILLAGE
TRIANGLE

E44

AL KHAIL RD

AL BARSHA
SOUTH 1

INTERNATIONAL
MEDIA PRODUCTION
ZONE (IMPZ)

AL BARSHA
SOUTH 4

JUMEIRAH VILLAGE
CIRCLE

AL BARSHA
SOUTH 2

ME'AISEM 1

JUMEIRAH
GOLF ESTATES

Norman
Clubhouse

E311

DUBAI
SPORTS CITY

AL BARSHA
SOUTH 3

DUBIOTECH

Miracle Garden

AL HEBIA 4

Dubai Autodrome

0   2km

N

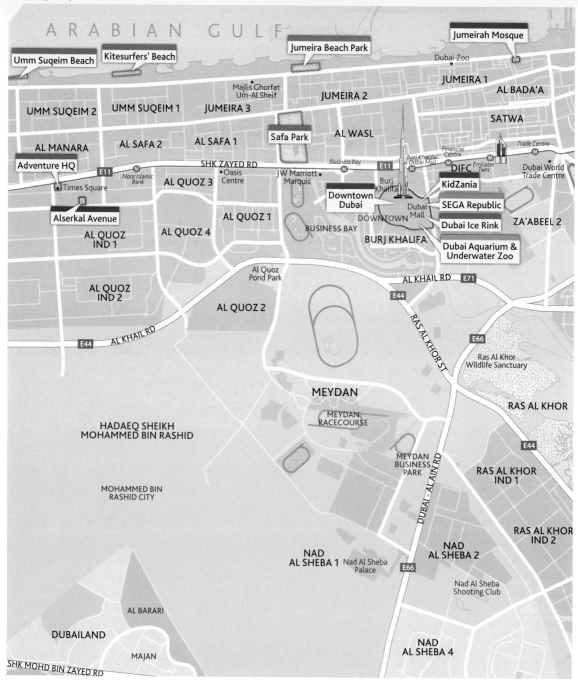

ARABIAN GULF

Umm Suqeim Beach

Kitesurfers' Beach

Jumeira Beach Park

Jumeirah Mosque

Dubai Zoo

Majlis Ghorfat
Um-Al Sheif

JUMEIRA 1

AL BADA'A

UMM SUQEIM 2

UMM SUQEIM 1

JUMEIRA 3

JUMEIRA 2

SATWA

AL WASL

Safa Park

Trade Centre

AL MANARA

AL SAFA 2

AL SAFA 1

Financial
Centre

Adventure HQ

SHK ZAYED RD

Burj Khalifa/
Dubai Mall

DIFC

Emirates
Twrs

Dubai World
Trade Centre

Noor Islamic
Bank

Oasis
Centre

Business Bay

E11

E11

KidZania

Times Square

AL QUOZ 3

JW Marriott
Marquis

Burj
Khalifa

SEGA Republic

Alserkal Avenue

Downtown
Dubai

Dubai Ice Rink

ZA'ABEEL 2

AL QUOZ 1

Dubai
Mall

AL QUOZ
IND 1

AL QUOZ 4

BUSINESS BAY

DOWNTOWN

Dubai Aquarium &
Underwater Zoo

BURJ KHALIFA

Al Quoz
Pond Park

AL KHAIL RD

E71

AL QUOZ
IND 2

AL QUOZ 2

E44

E66

RAS AL KHOR ST

Ras Al Khor
Wildlife Sanctuary

E44

AL KHAIL RD

MEYDAN

RAS AL KHOR

MEYDAN
RACECOURSE

HADAEQ SHEIKH
MOHAMMED BIN RASHID

MEYDAN
BUSINESS
PARK

RAS AL KHOR
IND 1

MOHAMMED BIN
RASHID CITY

DUBAI–AL AIN RD

E44

RAS AL KHOR
IND 2

NAD
AL SHEBA 2

NAD
AL SHEBA 1

Nad Al Sheba
Palace

E66

Nad Al Sheba
Shooting Club

AL BARARI

DUBAILAND

MAJAN

NAD
AL SHEBA 4

SHK MOHD BIN ZAYED RD

Sheikh Saeed Al Maktoum House

Heritage & Diving Villages

PALM DEIRA

AL MINA

Al Ghubaiba

Palm Deira

Hyatt Regency

Mamzar Beach Park

BUR DUBAI

Al Ras

DEIRA

CORNICHE DEIRA

HAMRIYA PORT

Dubai Museum

Al Fahidi

AL MURAR

Bur Dubai Boniyas Sq

AL MAMZAR

AL MANKHOOL

Al Fahidi Historical Neighbourhood

NAIF

AL BARAHA

ABU HAIL

AL JAFILIYA

Al Karama

Union

MUTEENA

Salah Al Din

AL WUHEIDA

Al Jafilya

Burjuman

AL RIGGA

Reef Mall

Century Mall

KARAMA

Dubai Creek

AL MURAQQABAT

Al Rigga

Abu Baker Al Siddque

HOR AL ANZ

Zabeel Park

ZA'ABEEL 1

Al Nasr Sports Club

Oud Metha

AL KHABAISI

Abu Hail

AL NAHDA 2

OUD METHA

Al Nasr Leisureland

Deira City Centre

AL ITTIHAD RD

Al Quiadah

Kids Connection

Deira City Centre

PORT SAEED

Stadium

Tee & Putt

Creek Park

Wafi

Healthcare City

AL TWAR 1

AL QUSAIS 1

AL NAHDA 1

AL QUSAIS IND 3

E66

E11

GGICO

Terminal 2

Al Nahda

Al Wasl Sports Club

Children's City

Al Jaddaf

AL QUSAIS IND 1

Emirates Kart Zone

Dubai Dolphinarium

Airport Terminal 1

DUBAI AIRPORT FREEZONE

Airport Freezone

AL QUSAIS IND 4

AL JADAF

CULTURE VILLAGE

GARHOUD

Airport Terminal 3

AL TWAR 2

AL QUSAIS IND 2

Drydock Jaddaf

Creek

DUBAI INTERNATIONAL AIRPORT

AL QUSAIS 2

Al Madina Mall

Festival Centre

Emirates

Al Qusais-1

Bowling City

MUHAISNAH 4

DUBAI FESTIVAL CITY

UMM RAMOOL

AL QUSAIS 3

Lulu Village

AL QUSAIS IND 5

AL BADIA

E71

Etisalat

THE LAGOON

AL TWAR 3

SHK MOHD BIN ZAYED RD

Rashidiya

E311

MUHAISNAH 2

AL RASHIDIYA

NADD AL HAMAR

AL REBAT ST

MUHAISNAH 1

iFLY Dubai

Little Explorers

Al Ittihad Mall

OUD AL MUTEENA 1

RAS AL KHOR IND 3

AL AWIR RD

Mirdif City Centre

MIRDIF

Aquaplay

Playnation

Uptown Mirdif

SHK MOHD BIN ZAYED RD

AL WARQA 2

AL MIZHAR 1

Wholesale Fruit & Vegetable Market

E311

AL WARQA 1

Mushrif Park

0   2km

SHARJAH EMIRATE

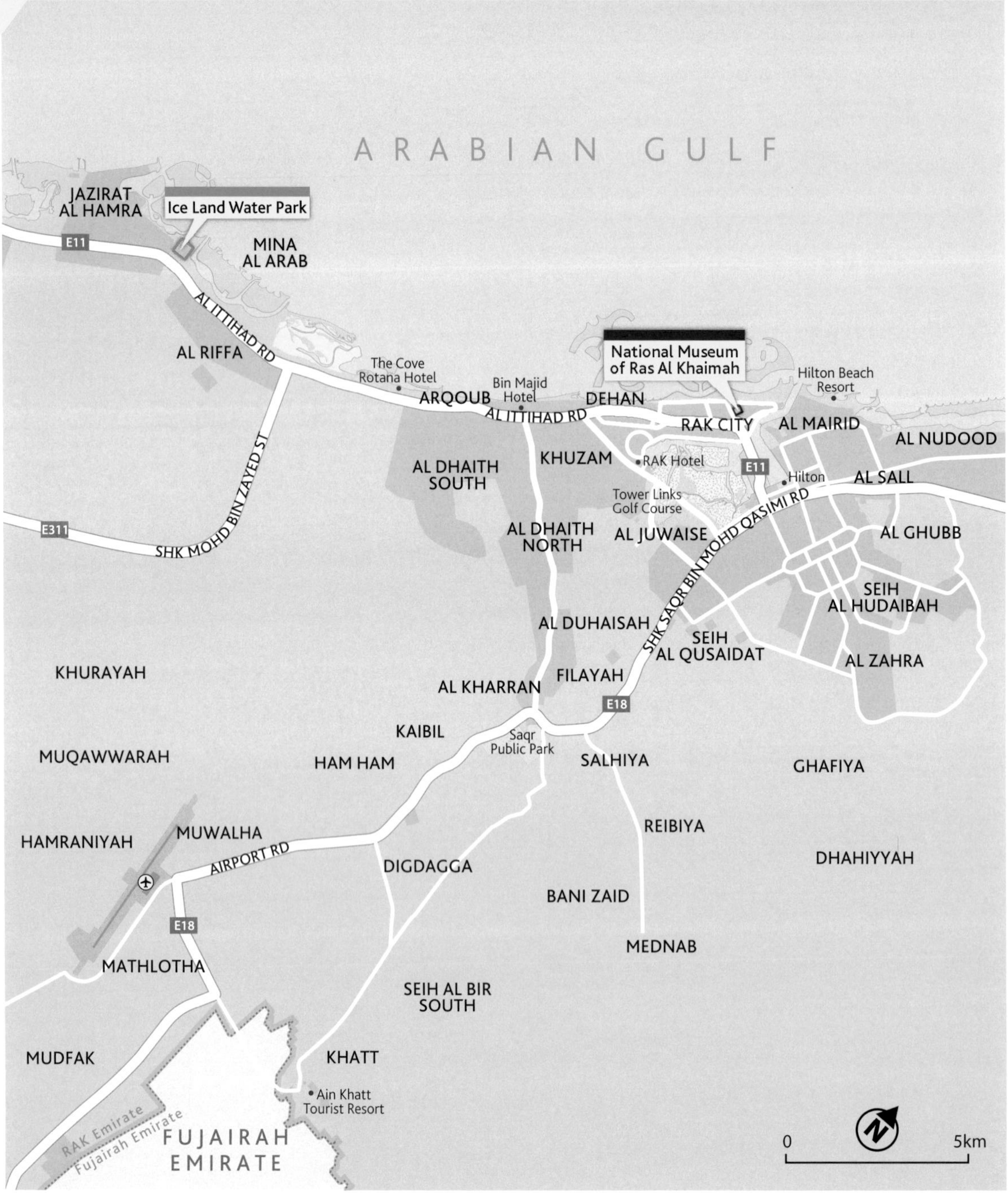

ARABIAN GULF

JAZIRAT
AL HAMRA

Ice Land Water Park

MINA
AL ARAB

E11

AL ITTIHAD RD

AL RIFFA

The Cove
Rotana Hotel

Bin Majid
Hotel

National Museum
of Ras Al Khaimah

Hilton Beach
Resort

ARQOUB

AL ITTIHAD RD

DEHAN

RAK CITY

AL MAIRID

AL NUDOOD

SHK MOHD BIN ZAYED ST

AL DHAITH
SOUTH

KHUZAM

RAK Hotel

AL SALL

E311

E311

SHK MOHD BIN ZAYED ST

Tower Links
Golf Course

Hilton

AL GHUBB

AL DHAITH
NORTH

AL JUWAISE

SEIH
AL HUDAIBAH

SHK SAQR BIN MOHD QASIMI RD

KHURAYAH

AL DUHAISAH

SEIH
AL QUSAIDAT

AL ZAHRA

AL KHARRAN

FILAYAH

KAIBIL

E18

MUQAWWARAH

HAM HAM

Saqr
Public Park

SALHIYA

GHAFIYA

HAMRANIYAH

MUWALHA

AIRPORT RD

REIBIYA

DHAHIYYAH

DIGDAGGA

BANI ZAID

E18

MEDNAB

MATHLOTHA

SEIH AL BIR
SOUTH

MUDFAK

KHATT

Ain Khatt
Tourist Resort

RAK Emirate
Fujairah Emirate

FUJAIRAH
EMIRATE

0   5km

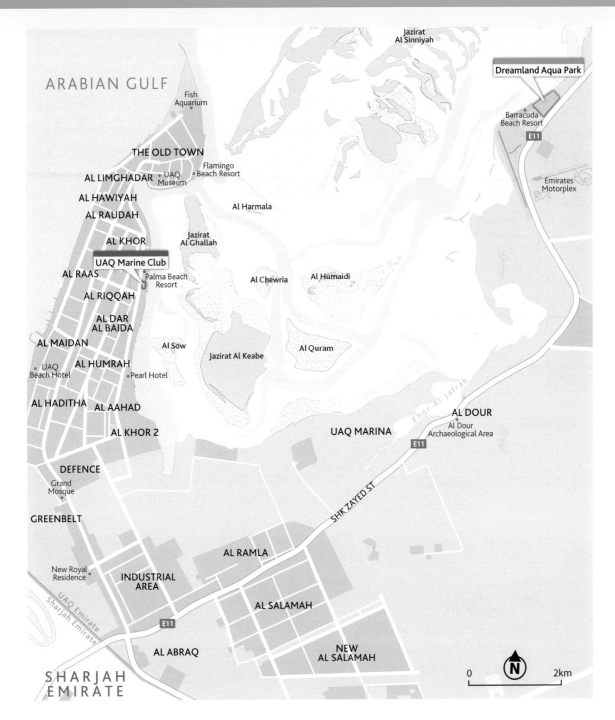

ARABIAN GULF

Jazirat
Al Sinniyah

Dreamland Aqua Park

Fish
Aquarium

Barracuda
Beach Resort

E11

THE OLD TOWN

AL LIMGHADAR

UAQ
Museum

Flamingo
Beach Resort

Emirates
Motorplex

AL HAWIYAH

AL RAUDAH

Al Harmala

AL KHOR

Jazirat
Al Ghallah

UAQ Marine Club

AL RAAS

Palma Beach
Resort

Al Chewria

Al Humaidi

AL RIQQAH

AL DAR
AL BAIDA

AL MAIDAN

Al Sow

Jazirat Al Keabe

Al Quram

UAQ
Beach Hotel

AL HUMRAH

Pearl Hotel

AL HADITHA

AL AAHAD

Khor Al Jafrah

AL DOUR

Al Dour
Archaeological Area

AL KHOR 2

UAQ MARINA

E11

DEFENCE

Grand
Mosque

GREENBELT

SHK ZAYED ST

AL RAMLA

New Royal
Residence

INDUSTRIAL
AREA

UAQ Emirate
Sharjah Emirate

AL SALAMAH

E11

AL ABRAQ

NEW
AL SALAMAH

SHARJAH
EMIRATE

0   N   2km

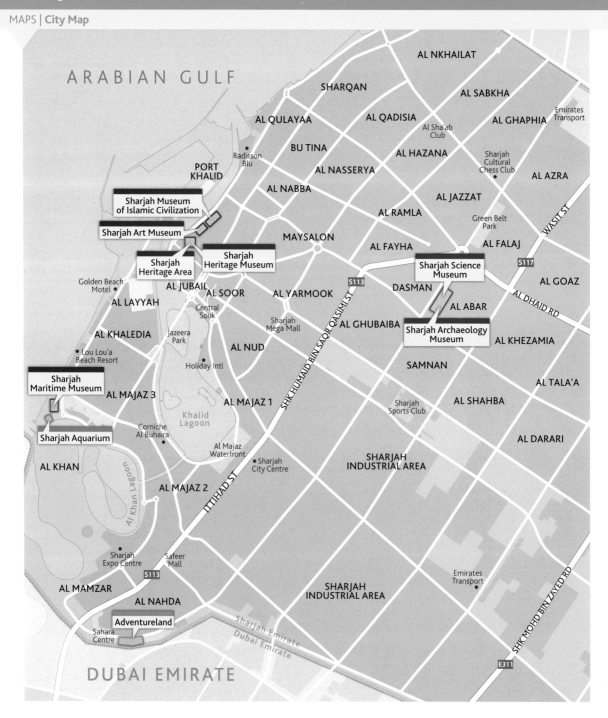

ARABIAN GULF

AL NKHAILAT

SHARQAN

AL SABKHA

AL QULAYAA

AL QADISIA

AL GHAPHIA

Emirates
Transport

Al Sha'ab
Club

PORT
KHALID

Radisson
Blu

BU TINA

AL HAZANA

Sharjah
Cultural
Chess Club

AL AZRA

AL NASSERYA

Sharjah Museum
of Islamic Civilization

AL NABBA

AL RAMLA

AL JAZZAT

Green Belt
Park

Sharjah Art Museum

MAYSALON

AL FAYHA

AL FALAJ

WASIT ST

Sharjah
Heritage Area

Sharjah
Heritage Museum

Sharjah Science
Museum

S117

Golden Beach
Motel

AL JUBAIL

AL SOOR

S113

DASMAN

AL DHAID RD

AL GOAZ

AL YARMOOK

AL ABAR

AL LAYYAH

Central
Souk

Sharjah
Mega Mall

AL GHUBAIBA

Sharjah Archaeology
Museum

AL KHEZAMIA

AL KHALEDIA

Jazeera
Park

AL NUD

SHK HUMAID BIN SAQR QASIMI ST

SAMNAN

AL TALA'A

Lou Lou'a
Beach Resort

Holiday Intl

Sharjah
Maritime Museum

AL MAJAZ 3

AL MAJAZ 1

Sharjah
Sports Club

AL SHAHBA

AL DARARI

Khalid
Lagoon

Sharjah Aquarium

Corniche
Al Buhaira

AL KHAN

Al Majaz
Waterfront

Sharjah
City Centre

SHARJAH
INDUSTRIAL
AREA

AL MAJAZ 2

ITTIHAD ST

Sharjah
Expo Centre

Safeer
Mall

S113

Emirates
Transport

SHARJAH
INDUSTRIAL AREA

AL MAMZAR

SHK MOHD BIN ZAYED RD

AL NAHDA

Adventureland

Sharjah Emirate

Sahara
Centre

Dubai Emirate

E311

DUBAI EMIRATE

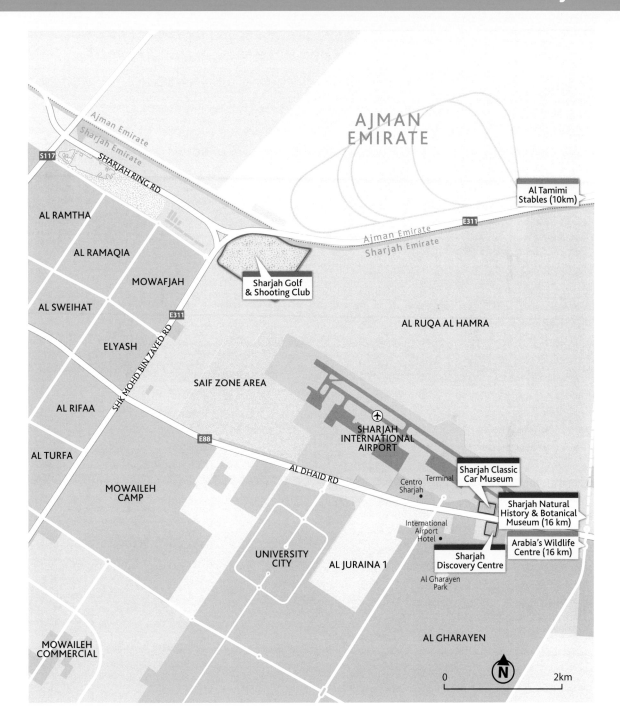

AJMAN EMIRATE

Ajman Emirate
Sharjah Emirate

S117

SHARJAH RING RD

AL RAMTHA

AL RAMAQIA

MOWAFJAH

AL SWEIHAT

ELYASH

E311

SHK MOHD BIN ZAYED RD

AL RIFAA

AL TURFA

SAIF ZONE AREA

E88

AL DHAID RD

MOWAILEH CAMP

MOWAILEH COMMERCIAL

UNIVERSITY CITY

AL JURAINA 1

Al Tamimi Stables (10km)

Ajman Emirate
Sharjah Emirate

E311

AL RUQA AL HAMRA

Sharjah Golf & Shooting Club

SHARJAH INTERNATIONAL AIRPORT

Centro Sharjah

Terminal

International Airport Hotel

Al Gharayen Park

AL GHARAYEN

Sharjah Classic Car Museum

Sharjah Natural History & Botanical Museum (16 km)

Arabia's Wildlife Centre (16 km)

Sharjah Discovery Centre

0   N   2km

INDEX

Residents' Guides

All you need to know about living in and loving some of the world's greatest cities and countries

 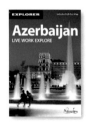 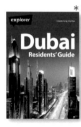  

Visitors' Guides

The perfect pocket-sized Visitors' Guides

Calendars

A whole year's worth of stunning images

Activity & Lifestyle Guides

Drive, trek, dive, sail and swim... life will never be boring again

Maps & Atlases

Never get lost, no matter where you are

Photography Books

Beautiful cities and countries caught through the lens

Off-Road Accessories

Your essential off-roading and camping gadgets

Retail Sales

Our products are available in most good bookshops as well as online at askexplorer.com/shop or Amazon.
Please contact retail@askexplorer.com

Bulk Sales & Customisation

All products are available for bulk purchase with customisation options. For discount rates and further information, please contact sales@askexplorer.com

Licensing & Digital Sales

All our content, maps and photography are available for print or digital use. For licensing enquiries, please contact licensing@askexplorer.com

Apps & eBooks

+ Also available as applications. Visit askexplorer.com/apps
* Now available in eBook format.
Visit askexplorer.com/shop or Amazon.

UAE Day Tripper

Lead Editor Stacey Siebritz
Section Editor Lily Lawes
Proofread by Fiona MacKenzie
Data managed by Amapola Castillo Baldo
Designed by Ieyad Charaf, Jayde Fernandes, Mohammed Shakkeer
Maps by Zainudheen Madathil, Dhanya Nellikkunnummal
Photographs by Pete Maloney, Hardy Mendrofa

Publishing
Chief Content Officer & Founder Alistair MacKenzie

Editorial
Managing Editor Carli Allan
Editor Laura Coughlin, Andy Mills, Kirsty Tuxford
Deputy Editor Lily Lawes, Stacey Siebritz
Production Coordinator Rahul Rajan
Editorial Assistant Amapola Castillo Baldo
Researchers Farida, Amrit Raj, Roja P, Praseena, Shahla Noura

Design & Photography
Creative Director Pete Maloney
Art Director Ieyad Charaf
Senior Designer Gary McGovern
Junior Designer M. Shakkeer
Layout Manager Jayde Fernandes
Cartography Manager Zain Madathil
Cartographer Noushad Madathil, Dhanya Nellikkunnummal, Ramla Kambravan, Shalu Sukumar
GIS Analyst Rafi KM, Hidayath Razi, Aslam
Photographer & Image Editor Hardy Mendrofa

Sales & Marketing
Director of Sales Peter Saxby
Media Sales Area Managers Sabrina Ahmed, Bryan Anes, Louise Burton, Adam Smith Matthew Whitbread, Laura Zuffova
Business Development Manager Pouneh Hafizi
Corporate Solutions Account Manager Vibeke Nurgberg
Director of Marketing Lindsay West
Senior Marketing Executive Stuart L. Cunningham
Director of Retail Ivan Rodrigues
Retail Sales Coordinator Michelle Mascarenhas
Retail Sales Area Supervisors Ahmed Mainodin, Firos Khan
Retail Sales Merchandisers Johny Mathew, Shan Kumar
Retail Sales Drivers Shabsir Madathil, Najumudeen K.I., Sujeer Khan
Warehouse Assistant Mohamed Haji

Finance, HR & Administration
Accountant Cherry Enriquez
Accounts Assistants Sunil Suvarna, Jeanette Carino Enecillo
Administrative Assistant Joy H. San Buenaventura
Reception Edelyn Isiderio
Public Relations Officer Rafi Jamal
Office Assistant Shafeer Ahamed
Office Manager – India Jithesh Kalathingal

IT & Digital Solutions
Digital Solutions Manager Derrick Pereira
Web Developer Mirza Ali Nasrullah
IT Manager R. Ajay
Database Programmer Pradeep T.P.

Contact Us

General Enquiries
We'd love to hear your thoughts and answer any questions you have about this book or any other Explorer product. Contact us at info@askexplorer.com

Careers
If you fancy yourself as an Explorer, send your CV (stating the position you're interested in) to jobs@askexplorer.com

Design & Contract Publishing
For enquiries about Explorer's Contract Publishing arm and design services, contact contracts@askexplorer.com

PR & Marketing
For PR and marketing enquiries contact marketing@askexplorer.com

Corporate Sales
For bulk sales and customisation options, for this book or any Explorer product, contact sales@askexplorer.com

Advertising & Sponsorship
For advertising and sponsorship, contact sales@askexplorer.com

Explorer Publishing & Distribution
PO Box 34275, Dubai, United Arab Emirates
askexplorer.com

Phone: +971 (0)4 340 8805
Fax: +971 (0)4 340 8806